DAD'S ARMY
The Making of a Television Legend

Bill Pertwee

DAVID & CHARLES
Newton Abbot London

"Excuse me, Mr. Benskin, but Mrs. White asked me to tell you that she ain't 'ad 'er bacon ration this week."

Wartime cartoon by George Morrow. *(Punch)*

DAD'S ARMY

British Library Cataloguing in
Publication Data
Pertwee, Bill
Dad's Army: the making of a
television legend.
1. Television programmes.
Comedies, 1950-1986
I. Title 791.45′5

ISBN 0-7153-9489-4

Typesetting by P.S. Typesetting
and printed in West Germany
by Mohndruck Gmb H

for David & Charles Publishers plc
Brunel House Newton Abbot Devon

DAD'S ARMY

CONTENTS

Member of the Home Guard: 'Tell Hitler not to come over tonight because the wife's cooking her carrot pudding'. (*Imperial War Museum, No. H12124*)

Introduction

There are certain moments in your life you remember as milestones and one such moment in mine was receiving a phone call in the summer of 1968 from BBC producer David Croft offering me two lines as an air raid warden in a new television series called *Dad's Army*. Until then I had been involved mainly in radio, summer shows and cabaret, but suddenly I found myself in the company of a delightfully warm group of film, television and stage actors, all of us being in on the start of what was to become one of the great television programmes this country has produced. *Dad's Army* became beloved by the viewing public, including the Royal Family, and was eventually adapted into a long-running radio series, a stage musical – including an appearance in a Royal Command Performance in the presence of Her Majesty the Queen at the London Palladium – and a full-length feature film made by Columbia Pictures. This book is not just the story of a successful television series of eighty episodes that were made over nine years, but also a story about the families and friends of those actors who became legends in their own lifetimes.

The words 'Dad's Army' are now part of history and the English language. The idea of presenting a programme about the Home Guard was conceived by Jimmy Perry who had been a member of this corps in his teens before he enlisted in the Army. One day in the late Sixties when he was working as an actor in the theatre he cast his mind back to those days in the Home Guard and thought that the subject might be presented on television – after all, nobody had done it before. Perhaps nobody had thought about it before or if they had, the idea probably seemed ridiculous. Who would be interested in a television programme about a group of generally senior citizens trying to look like soldiers, guarding their country with pitchforks, broomsticks and any other items of domestic hardware they could lay their hands on? But wasn't it the exceptional optimism of those loyal countrymen that might prove to be the catalyst for the television public to latch onto? The original concept of the Home Guard – Local Defence Volunteers as they were first called – had been deadly serious even though their weapons were primitive.

This Leslie Baker cartoon pokes fun at the shortage of uniforms suffered by the Home Guard when it was first formed. *(Punch)*

" I've laid your uniform out, my Lord."

'They don't like it up 'em'

Reminiscing in this way Jimmy Perry realised that here was a ready-made comedy situation, one that could be written about without in any way belittling the efforts of the Guard.

When Anthony Eden made his historic speech in June 1940, calling for men under and over the age of active service in the armed forces to form a local defence corps, there was an immediate response from every eligible male in the country. Britain had been rearming for some time for what Prime Minister Neville Chamberlain knew was inevitable. Chamberlain had had many meetings with Hitler and knew that the German Leader could never be trusted to keep his word. This was reflected in the Prime Minister's private letters to his son from Germany just before the outbreak of war. Czech-

'A Home Guard weapon was one that was dangerous to the enemy, and to a greater degree, to the operator' — *Lieut.-Colonel J. Lee, Early Days in the Home Guard.*

(Independent Free Press.)

oslovakia had been sacrificed in 1938 for which many people never forgave Chamberlain. He knew only too well that the piece of paper he waved in the air on his return from Munich in 1938 that promised the British people 'peace in our time' was just one more promise that Hitler would break. In 1938 the armaments factories went into full production, but by 1940 we had been driven out of France and the Low Countries, together with many allied armies, and the British needed not only material rearmament but also a psychological uplift. In 1940 Winston Churchill, who was now Prime Minister in charge of a coalition government, told the British people that they would fight on the beaches and never surrender; but his master stroke was to ask all those men not fit for active service to form

Above: **Captain Mainwaring: 'Right then, pay attention, men'. Our boys ready for action.** *(Michael Fresco)*

Below: **'War or no war, you can't leave that van here' — An AA patrolman antagonizes Captain Mainwaring by failing to grasp the military importance of the Walmington-on-Sea Home Guard.** *(Columbia Pictures Industries Inc.)*

themselves into a Home Guard as his request boosted the flagging morale of the country. Many families had already been touched by war. Husbands, sons and sweethearts had left the comfort of their homes for the rigours of battle. Some had already perished or been taken prisoner in the fighting in France, and the Navy had endured horrific losses at sea. But in Britain itself, every home was to be involved in the war with the formation of the Local Defence Volunteers. Houses, pubs, village halls and the like became the headquarters of Britain's new 'fighting force'. It says a great deal for the sincerity of the men and their involvement in the war effort that the British people felt that they could sleep easy in their beds at night with the 'boys', albeit

Above: **'Right, broomsticks and pitchforks at the ready, men'** *(Columbia Pictures Industries Inc.)*

Below: **It's a good job we all use Persil . . . The newly formed platoon keeping fit for the fight — even though the rest of the uniform hasn't arrived!** *(Columbia Pictures Industries Inc.)*

Bill Cotton, then Head of Variety at the BBC.

most of them 'old boys', watching over them, even though some people must have had doubts as to the Home Guard's ability to cope with the expected German invasion from land, sea and air when they had only pitchforks, broomsticks and, if they were lucky, a shot-gun and a few cartridges between them.

It was with these thoughts that Jimmy Perry returned home one day in the late Sixties and contacted producer/director David Croft, for whom he had worked on a few television programmes, and asked if it would be possible to create a series about the Home Guard. Perhaps Jimmy had remembered a very funny radio comedian called Robb Wilton – very much a Captain Mainwaring – who in the 1940s had caricatured the Home Guard with his joke that began

> 6The day I joined the Home Guard my missus said to me, 'What are you?' I said, 'I'm one of the Home Guard.' She said, 'What do you do?' I said, 'I've got to stop Hitler's Army from landing.' She said, 'What, just you?' I said "Oh no, there's me and Charlie Evans and Harry Bates, and ... well, there's seven or eight of us altogether.' She said, 'Do you know this feller Hitler?' I said, 'Of course not.' She said, 'Well, how will you know if it's him if he lands?' I said, 'Well, I've got a tongue in me head haven't I?9

Remembering the very good reaction that Robb Wilton had had in making gentle fun of the Home Guard, might have prompted Jimmy and David to take the thought of creating a series about Dad's Army seriously and to hurry to the typewriter.

Although the BBC programme makers had commissioned Jimmy and

David to write an initial short series of scripts about the Home Guard, there was some doubt in their minds that a comedy programme based on this subject would prove successful. The then Head of Variety was Bill Cotton, son of one of Britain's best loved Band Leaders Billy Cotton of 'Wakey, Wakey' fame, who said of Dad's Army:

> 6As with all great comedies, Dad's Army had the first qualifications of a smash hit. It was very well written and cleverly cast. Huw Weldon always used to tell the story of being confused whilst watching the show being rehearsed – he thought Arthur Lowe would be the Sergeant and John Le Mesurier would be the officer. He considered reversing it to be a stroke of genius. Dad's Army to me was a wonderful surprise. When David Croft told me he wanted to do a comedy about the Home Guard I told him he was out of his head. I am very grateful I was not heeded. In fact, in later years I had the enormous joy of travelling to Thetford, where they were filming, to tell the cast they had topped the ratings with an audience of 21 million. Dad's Army, in my opinion, is a wonderful document of social history – it captures so much of the atmosphere of the Second World War. I am positive that in a hundred years' time people will be watching it to get a feel of the period, probably in preference to the mass of factual material that will be available.
>
> Meanwhile, I am sure we will be kept in touch with Walmington-on-Sea with seasons of repeats. If we don't, I'll write and complain!9

The Home Guard and Molotov Cocktails

'On one occasion a platoon commander had just thrown one of these missiles and was explaining to his men that they were foolproof ... Private Buggins stepped forward from the ranks, halted three paces from the platoon commander and saluted smartly. 'Yes Buggins?' 'Excuse me, sir, your breeches are on fire!' – quoted by Norman Longmate in *The Real Dad's Army*

The Creators

Jimmy Perry, OBE

If a small boy's sole ambition is to own a full suit of white tie and tails, a pair of riding breeches and a trilby hat and to adorn the whole outfit with a pipe, you can be sure that sooner or later the young man in question will make the entertainment industry sit up and take notice. Although few people at the age of five or six know exactly what they want to do when they grow up, Jimmy Perry certainly did. Looking back he says: 'I had no family inheritance of show business. My father was in antiques and I got very bored hearing them discussed from morning to night.' Some of that talk of antiquity must have rubbed off on young Jimmy because he is now very knowledgeable on the subject.

'I was taken to the theatre by my mother as a very small boy and was immediately smitten by this wonderful world of bright lights, extrovert people and exciting atmosphere. We went to see plays, and the great variety comedians of the day in music halls in and around London. We went to the cinema and I used to come home and re-enact whole scenes in front of the mirror. One particular film I saw was *The Sacred Flame* and that really got me. I was taken to a pantomime when I was seven and when we got home I sulked for two hours because I hadn't wanted it to end. I lived in a complete world of fantasy, I hated school and particularly one of the masters who was a nasty piece of work. I pretended I was a member of the Secret Service and I went to the headmaster and told him that the nasty piece of work was a German spy and must be sacked. I hated all sport – cricket, football and rugby – but I was a very good athlete and could run faster than most of the other boys. I knew even as a young teenager that I wanted to act, I wanted to wear smart clothes and go out with beautiful women. I tried to grow a moustache but this was a failure, so was the pipe I tried to smoke! When the war started I wanted to get into uniform, but I had to wait until the summer of 1940 when I joined the Home Guard in Barnes where we lived. I loved going out on the common and doing night duty and I had no fear of being killed by the bombing which had already flattened the school I had attended. My mother was always fearful of me being out at night during the air raids and catching cold (shades of Private Pike), but I enjoyed it.'

Jimmy Perry, who hit on the idea of writing a comedy series about the Home Guard.

WINDSOR HOUSE ENTERTAINMENT STAFF, BUTLIN'S HOLIDAY CAMP, PWLLHELI

Jimmy Perry during his season as a Butlin redcoat (standing third from right). *(Jimmy Perry)*

After being bombed out, Jimmy and his family moved to Watford and that town was eventually to play an important part in his life and, to a lesser extent, *Dad's Army.* He once again joined the Home Guard in that area and waited for his call up into the Army, but before that could happen he was drafted into a munitions factory. In 1943 Jimmy became Gunner Perry of the Royal Artillery and was posted to Oswestry. He immediately asked who ran the Base Concert Party and said that if they didn't have one perhaps he should start one. A concert party was not the uppermost thought in the commanding officer's mind at that time as there were more serious and pressing problems to be dealt with, such as Hitler and preparation for the second front. However, Gunner Perry had to be listened to and the concert party of Oswestry was organised with Perry to the fore who now had an outlet for doing some public entertain-

ment, which by now included impressions of Ned Sparks, Gordon Harker, President Roosevelt, Winston Churchill and Robb Wilton, all of whom were currently known by the young soldiers in the audiences. Jimmy had previously won a talent contest at a Gaumont Cinema and the Army was now receiving the full force of his personality. He included such jokes as 'I believed in free love until I woke up this morning and found my wallet missing.' This joke was quite risky and daring (especially as at that time he hardly even knew the facts of life) but his audience laughed and to Jimmy laughter and applause were becoming an essential part of his life.

One day there was upheaval in the Camp when practically all of the personnel were sent south in preparation for the D-Day invasion of Europe. Only a handful, including Gunner Perry, remained behind. Did the Second Front in

France not need a Concert Party? What would Eisenhower and Montgomery do without impressions of Ned Sparks and Gordon Harker! As it happened most of the battalion were cut to pieces on the beaches of Normandy, so Jimmy had escaped that bloody conflict.

One night, a captain at the Camp who had now taken over compèring the shows, was very drunk and Jimmy complained bitterly about his unprofessional conduct on stage. The captain immediately took revenge on Jimmy and had him posted to the Far East, and so another chapter in the life of Gunner Perry began.

At some point Jimmy climbed the ranks to Sergeant but for the sake of this narrative we'll stick to 'Gunner'. The unit left Liverpool in a convoy of fifty ships and travelled via America, and not the Mediterranean, because of the threat of attack by German U-boats. This was very worrying for everyone involved in that convoy – everyone, that is, except Gunner Perry who was far more concerned that the ship did not have a concert party. Was this huge vessel with its captive audience also going to be deprived of Ned Sparks and Gordon Harker? After a short stay at Cape Town, the ship arrived at Bombay, five weeks after leaving Liverpool. From Bombay Jimmy was posted to an anti-aircraft unit at Deolali, then to Assam in the jungle. This was Jimmy's opportunity to form an entertainment unit and to give the Far East a taste of his impressions. Many years later, the memory of that period of entertainment in the jungle and all it meant to those troops became the basis for the television series *It aint 'alf 'ot Mum!*. In 1945 the atom bomb was dropped on Japan and the war in the Far East was over, but there were plenty of Japanese soldiers who were still carrying on their own private war in that area. Jimmy became ill and was sent back to Deolali. In 1946 he was sent to Delhi where he joined one of the renowned Gang Shows which were in the process of being amalgamated with the Combined Services Entertainment Unit (CSE as it was known for many years after). Indian Independence was now on the horizon and Indians themselves were being killed and wounded in the turmoil. The week before independence Jimmy left India on the *SS Franconia* together with hundreds of other troops. They docked at Southampton and shortly afterwards he was demobbed during the freezing winter of 1947.

At that time Jimmy weighed a meagre $8\frac{1}{2}$ stone and spent

Below: **Jimmy Perry as 'Charley's Aunt' (sitting centre) with his wife, Gilda Perry on his right, in the stage production of** *Charley's Aunt,* **Palace Theatre, Watford, 1958.** *(Jimmy Perry)*

three months sitting in front of the open fire at his parents' home. He now had to decide about his future and felt that his chosen course was a career in the theatre. He went to see an old friend who was appearing at Collins Music Hall in Islington and before long Jimmy was back smelling the greasepaint. He was coached in drama by an old army mate Joe O'Connor and then applied for and won a scholarship to the Royal Academy of Dramatic Art in London. During his training at RADA he met and worked with other aspiring actors and actresses, including Robert Shaw, Joan Collins, Lawrence Harvey, Lionel Jeffries, Warren Mitchell and Dorothy Tutin.

Jimmy was now on his way as a professional performer. During the summer holidays from RADA he did seasons at Butlin's holiday camps as a singer and feed to the comics. In 1952 he joined the cast of *Glorious Days*, which starred

**'What are the silly asses up to now?':
Jimmy Perry and
David Croft.** (*Bill
Pertwee*)

Anna Neagle, at the Palace Theatre. Anna played Florence Nightingale, Nell Gwynn and Queen Victoria in a series of historical cameos. There was a cast of seventy-five and among the dancers was a nineteen-year-old, Gilda; she and Jimmy hit it off together and were married in 1953. Jimmy meanwhile had a part in A.P. Herbert's *Water Gipsies* at the Winter Gardens Theatre. Repertory in Richmond and Watford followed and Jimmy and Gilda then took over the lease of the Palace Theatre, Watford. A very young pair of actor/actress/managers now had to keep the theatre open for fifty-two weeks of the year with weekly rep. This they did as well as putting on an annual pantomine, the revenue of which kept their heads above water for the rest of the year. It was from this period that Jimmy remembered a number of actors who had appeared at Watford and suggested their names for the *Dad's Army* cast. Eventually Jimmy and Gilda succeeded in persuading Watford Council to take over the Palace Theatre and to run it as a civic trust. It could now be properly funded and not have to rely constantly on the box office to keep it open, which had always been a huge task. The one draw-back was that Watford Corporation did not want Jimmy and Gilda to be a part of the new set-up, so they were paid off.

In 1965 Jimmy and Gilda moved back to London and found a flat in Westminster where they still live. Gilda went off to do summer revues and Jimmy toured for quite a long period with John Hanson in *When You're Young*. This was followed by a tour in *Seagulls over Sorrento* in which he met author Hugh Hasting, who would later be involved with *Dad's Army*. Jimmy then spent two years with the producer/director Joan Littlewood at

the Theatre Royal, Stratford East and during this period the idea for *Dad's Army* began to develop. Jimmy had done one or two television shows for producer/director David Croft and he took his idea to him. David liked it and it was decided that they should collaborate in writing the script. That decision was the start of a long and successful partnership in which they were to create some of the most popular television productions of the Sixties, Seventies and Eighties. Jimmy wrote the *Dad's Army* signature tune 'Who do you think you are kidding Mr Hitler?' which won the Ivor Novello award in 1970 for the best signature tune. It captures the sound of the period so well that many people believe it was actually written in the Forties which is understandable because it was recorded by Bud Flanagan who was a famous musical hall entertainer and recording name of the Forties and Fifties along with his partner Chesney Allen. Recording the signature tune was, in fact, the last engagement that Bud

Flanagan undertook, and his voice totally captures the atmosphere of the war years. Jimmy also wrote the title music for *It aint 'alf 'ot Mum!* and *Hi-De-Hi.* Jimmy's solo writing achievements for television series include *The Gnomes of Dulwich* for the BBC, *Lollipop* for ATV, and *The Old Boy Network* and three series of *Turns* for the BBC. *Turns* was a compilation of film clips of some of the great variety and music hall turns (a music hall performer was always known as a turn) of the past. The research involved in finding these old film clips in archives all over London and then writing the linking material was a labour of love for Jimmy. Some of his research unearthed unique film material that had not been seen since its origination. Talking to him about the music hall, one is left with the feeling that he would have liked to have been a turn on the variety circuit himself. Fortunately however, his career went in other directions, for otherwise the viewing public would have been deprived of some of Britain's outstanding television comedy.

David Croft, OBE

I have often tried to think who David Croft reminds me of and only recently have I realised who it was. As a small boy I was part of a group of pranksters, scrumping apples, putting glue on bicycle handlebars and indulging in other silly activities. One of the group, Henry, was the motivator; he would set us up, then stand back when we got in a fix and laugh unashamedly.

I can see him now, his shoulders heaving, the sound of his laughter 'tee-hee-hee' and the drawing in of breath with a hissing sound. We, the gang, got as much fun out of Henry's laughter as he got out of getting us into trouble.

David Croft is like Henry, because the actors and actresses in his productions are the gang who get into trouble in situations that he and his co-writers have created. He loves watching a comedy situation develop and will 'tee-hee' each time the gag is repeated at rehearsals, much to the delight of the cast. One can be sure that millions of viewers are going to be laughing too when the programme is screened.

I have known David for well over twenty years and he has always had a slight smile in his eyes, probably because he loves comedy and, more importantly, loves life. A fairly serious illness a few years ago

David Croft, television director, producer and writer (with Jimmy Perry) of *Dad's Army.*

appears to have been just shrugged off as a temporary nuisance. David works hard, is disciplined, and has the good sense to surround himself with an efficient workforce. I am sure he would agree that the teaming up with Jimmy Perry was another very important milestone in his life. *Dad's Army* was, after all, the beginning of a hugely successful period of writing and production for them both.

David was already a very experienced director/producer long before 1968, with the highly rated *Hugh and I, Beggar My Neighbour* and *This is Your Life* for BBC TV. All his experience has been gathered from a career that started with his parents, Anne Croft and Reginald Sharland (the family name), who were two big stars of the Twenties and Thirties. They were both starring at the Hippodrome Theatre in London while baby David slept in a prop basket; their dressing-room was his nursery. At the age of four, he wandered accidentally on to the stage at the old Shaftesbury Theatre where his parents were playing. David's mother was also a

theatrical manager and at the age of sixteen he was negotiating percentages with theatre managers on her behalf. There was, of course, no doubt that the entertainment business was to be his career and this promise was soon to be fulfilled when he took the part of the butcher's boy in the 1938 film *Goodbye Mr Chips*, starring Robert Donat.

When war broke out in 1939 David became an air raid warden and in 1942 he joined the Royal Artillery in a light 'ack-ack' regiment and was posted to the 1st Army in North Africa. In 1944 he transferred to the Dorset Regiment and saw service in India and Malaya. He eventually became a major and worked with General Mongomery's staff at the War Office as hostilities drew to a close.

After the war, David was soon back on the boards with repertory at Wolverhampton and Hereford. He appeared in the London production of the musical *Wild Violets* and toured with *Belinda Fair* and *The Belle of New York*. He met his future wife Ann at the first rehearsal of *The Belle* in Mac's

A social evening at Thetford. Why is David Croft wearing a dinner suit?
L to R: Joan Lowe (back to the camera), the author, Ann Croft, David Croft, Arthur Lowe
(Montague)

rehearsal studio in Windmill Street. He was playing Harry Bronson, a playboy millionaire and had to wear a lurid tail suit. Ann was understudying the leading lady. They married a year later.

At about this time David started to write in earnest with a collaborator, musician Cyril Ornadel. This union proved to be a very worthwhile partnership. David's lyrics and Cyril's music were a feature of many a lavish production at the London Palladium, the Howard and Wyndham Group, and at the Alexandra Theatre, Birmingham. The 'Alex', as it is always known, was then under the management of that fine man of the theatre (and cricket addict!) Derek Salberg, a friend to many thespians.

David sang for a while with the BBC Show Band Singers and backed many international stars, both on radio and on record. He then decided to enter the arena of television and became a script editor at Rediffusion Television, then moved up to Tyne-Tees TV, which was headed at that time by the legendary George and Alfred Black. It was at Tyne-Tees TV that David learned his craft for all his future work on the small screen. Writing and directing at Tyne-Tees brought him into contact with some of the people he would be associated with in the future – Mollie Sugden, Jack Haig, William Moore, etc.

David eventually moved back to London and for a short time became production manager for the Richard Stone Organisation (Richard was by then his agent), producing the Butlin's revue shows at their holiday camps up and down the country. A meeting with Eric Maschwitz, then one of the controllers of BBC TV, resulted in his moving over to the Corporation as a television director, where he has been ever since. He directed the early Benny Hill shows (by his own admission not very successfully) and then other programmes which set him on his present path to success. An early lesson in camera techniques and angles was demonstrated to him by a director who used three coins on a table to represent the three cameras and moved them about in a very simple way. It is rather more complicated today but the principle remains the same and when David showed me how it was done I understood exactly what he meant.

People have said 'He's a hard-headed businessman' or 'He understands actors, having been one' or 'He's his own best casting director', but without exception I believe they would all say that he was very good at his job. One doesn't co-write, produce and direct eighty episodes of *Dad's Army*, fifty-six episodes of *It ain't 'alf 'ot Mum!*, fifty-eight episodes of *Hi-De-Hi*, sixty-nine episodes of *Are You Being Served?* and, to date, sixty episodes of *'Allo 'allo* without some knowledge of the business. In co-operation with just two other writers, David has been resposible for this phenomenal output for the past twenty-one years. Not a bad record in anybody's book.

David's achievements were recognised when he won the Desmond Davis award for outstanding contributions to television and it was very fitting that the person announcing this award, at a large gathering of fellow professionals, was Arthur Lowe.

David's personal and social life is very full. He and his wife Ann have a large family, one of whom, his daughter Penny, has followed him into television script-writing. To spend time with David over a meal and a few bottles of wine is always a jolly affair and you can bet your life there will be plenty of tee-heeing going on!

Since the war began, the government have received countless inquiries from all over the kingdom from men of all ages who are, for one reason or another, not at present engaged in military service, and who wish to do something for the defence of their country. Well, now is your opportunity. We want large numbers of such men in Great Britain, who are British subjects, between the ages of seventeen and sixty five ... to come forward and offer their services ... The name of the new Force which is now to be raised will be 'The Local Defence Volunteers' – Anthony Eden, *radio broadcast, Tuesday 14th May, 1940*

Casting the Net

Relaxing during the filming of 'Enemy at the Gates' L to R: Arnold Ridley/Private Godfrey; Ian Lavender/ Private Pike; Arthur Lowe/Captain Mainwaring; Clive Dunn/Corporal Jones; John Le Mesurier/Sgt. Wilson; James Beck/Private Walker

As with any period television or film production the initial research is very important. It is a painstaking and arduous business, but never dull and extremely rewarding. In the case of *Dad's Army*, David Croft, Jimmy Perry and the BBC paid attention to even the smallest detail. Among the details that had to be discussed and researched before even a word of script was written were the sort of clothes that were worn in the 1940s and vehicles of the period – cars, buses, vans and motor-cycles. All the vehicles had to be obtained in a roadworthy condition as they were to be used in the programmes for real. Cigarette packets, sweet wrappers, newspapers, magazines and hairstyles of

'I can always find you a little something in spite of the rationing, Mr. Yeatman'.
(Bill Pertwee)

the period and the sort of food that was eaten during the war all had to be researched. Wartime recipes were found, most of which were based on simple ingredients such as beetroot, carrots, potatoes, dried egg-powder, cheese and fat bacon pieces (when they could be obtained), oatmeal, parsnips, apples, dried fish from Scandinavia (a fish-cake was a real luxury) and rabbit (Flanagan and Allan had a popular song about them) and a lot of ingenuity. Most of the foods that were taken for granted before the war were rationed and became extremely scarce, and were obtainable only on the black market and even then in small quantities.

Some typical and popular dishes of that period included Fish in Savoury Custard, Pathfinder Pudding, Carrot Jam, Pilchard Layer Loaf, Vinegar Cake, Belted Leeks, Rabbit Surprise and the best known of all, Woolton Pie. Recipes for some of these dishes can be found at the end of the book. These curtailed menus obviously did no harm to the nation's health because it was a fact that people were healthier in wartime than at almost any other period.

A great amount of time was spent on researching the weapons the Home Guard used over a period of several years, from the early broom-sticks and pick-axe handles, to the later American World War I P17 rifles that were sent by President Roosevelt, the Chicago gangster-type tommy guns, and much later the British-made Sten gun, which became a great luxury even though it was in short supply. When they arrived in Britain, the American consignment of weapons were covered in layers of thick grease as the majority had been in store for years.

Not least of the problems to be faced by David Croft and Jimmy Perry was casting the seven

'I was earning about nine pounds a week in repertory when someone saw me and contacted David Croft to tell him that I looked stupid enough to play Private Pike.' – Ian Lavender

main characters who would feature in the Walmington-on-Sea Home Guard. The eventual casting was brilliant. The first character to be decided was Captain Mainwaring.

David Croft:

❝ I had various people in mind, but hadn't given anyone serious thought at that early stage. Jimmy Perry was very keen at the outset for Arthur Lowe to play Mainwaring, but there were one or two people at the BBC who had doubts about it, saying 'he doesn't work for us' (a reference to his long contract in *Coronation Street* and *Pardon the Expression* for Granada TV). We arranged lunch at the BBC to discuss the idea with Arthur, but it didn't get off to a very good start. Arthur said 'I hope it's not going to be one of those silly programmes like *Hugh and I*, I can't stand it!'. I had to say I was the director of that programme, at which he was slightly taken aback. Luckily it all resolved itself and our first casting was complete. **❞**

Jimmy Perry:

❝ Michael Mills, the Head of Situation Comedy at the BBC at that time, wanted David to seriously consider John Le Mesurier for the Sergeant and with John's long experience in films this seemed a good idea. Michael also suggested Clive Dunn to play Corporal Jones. I didn't know much about Clive then, but when I see some of the videos of the programme now he makes me laugh a lot.

Michael was also responsible for renaming the programme. I knew my working title *The Fighting*

Tigers was not right and Michael came up with the brilliant *Dad's Army.'*

David cast Arnold Ridley, who had worked with him before in television, Ian Lavender (with the help of David's wife who had seen this 'young lad' in a play), and Jimmy Beck.**'**

David Croft:

'It was Michael Mills again who suggested that John Laurie was available and would be great for Private Frazer, who initially was a retired seafarer in the series, but later became the Walmington-on-Sea undertaker.

Jimmy and I were both delighted to have John. After all he had been a fine stage actor in his time, and played in many prestigious films.**'**

Jimmy Perry:

'Very early in the series John made us both laugh when he said 'You know, I think you and David are illiterate [hc was probably referring to some light-hearted conversation we were having at the time]. I have played every major Shakespearean role in the theatre and I'm considered the finest speaker of verse in the country, and I end up becoming famous doing this crap!' This remark did nothing to diminish our great admiration for John!

David cast Bill Pertwee and Edward Sinclair, and I suggested Frank Williams.**'**

David and Jimmy were presented with the Writers Guild Award for three consecutive years in 1969-71 and also the BAFTA Award in 1971 for Best Television Situation Comedy Programme. In 1978 they donned morning suits for a trip to Buckingham Palace to each collect their O.B.E., awarded in the Queen's Birthday Honours List.

Jimmy Perry and David Croft after receiving their OBE's from H.M. the Queen in 1976 *(Press Association Ltd)*

The man and the hour: Captain Mainwaring. *(BBC)*

The Magnificent Seven

Arthur Lowe

During the nine-year run of *Dad's Army* I got to know everyone connected with the production very well, some more than others.

Arthur Lowe fascinated me from the first day I met him. In rehearsals, you wondered how he could make everyone laugh so much, not just the rest of the cast but also the technicians, with such little effort on his part. Naturally, the script writers were involved in this laughter, for it was their job to create the funny situations, but even they could be surprised by Arthur's extra lift of the eyebrow or movement of the hand that had not been there at a previous run-through. He was, you see, a natural humorist, not a manu-factured actor. He had had his fair share of repertory theatre, with seasons of weekly productions up and down the country, where his natural instincts had been honed and sharpened. His dialogue in the comedy situation was punctu-ated by a word started in a hesitant fashion and then continued in a firmer way to make his point. Originally this was probably done to focus the audience's attention on to him – but then it had become a habit. Sometimes it seemed that he was collecting his thoughts before continuing. But whatever the reason, Arthur made it a natural part of the character he was por-traying. His long pauses before he made a comment were superbly timed. Occasionally it seemed that he had paused too long, but seldom was he proved wrong.

As I got to know Arthur the man more and more it became obvious that Mainwaring had been waiting for him, and Arthur for Mainwaring. The two fitted like a split screen merging into one. The first time I dined with Arthur in a restaurant, he said to the waiter, 'The Warden will sort out the bill.' This was clearly Mainwaring the character overlapping with Arthur the man and he was fully aware that this remark would amuse the other diners. Offstage, Arthur could be quite a private person. It was his belief that the mystique of the theatre should be left on the stage and that it was the public's place to observe from afar. He therefore disliked engaging in theatre chat with autograph hunters.

Not only was I sympathetic with these views, but Arthur and I had other things in common. He, like myself, was a late starter in the acting profession, and we were both avid cricket fans. He knew that I liked messing about in boats, particularly in harbours, and my wife and I spent several relaxed days with Arthur and his wife Joan on board their steam yacht *Amazon*. They had bought the boat in a very rough condition and, with the aid of original plans and photographs from the Maritime Museum at Greenwich, had set about restoring it to its original glory. During some of the early rehearsals of *Dad's Army*, Arthur would spend his spare moments por-ing over the restoration plans so that he could make the necessary preparations to make the craft seaworthy. All the interior fittings were suit-ably chosen and the result was superb. Arthur and Joan gave some wonderful parties on board the boat and Arthur took great pleasure in walking around the deck in his yacht-ing cap and with a gin and

'You stupid boy'

French in his hand, showing everyone around. He had, in fact, wanted to join the Navy, but his eyesight was not sufficiently good, so his war service was in the Army. The *Amazon* is now in the capable hands of Arthur's son Stephen whose maritime training was carried out in the Merchant

acquired a few of Sandy Powell's mannerisms. Sandy used to make long pauses, raise his glasses slightly and then give a little cough before commenting on whatever was going on around him. When Arthur was acting, though, instead of raising his glasses he would rub his hand over

Arthur and Joan Lowe aboard their steam yacht 'Amazon'
(Joan Lowe)

Navy. Stephen also had a spell as an oil rig deep-sea diver until an accident forced him to give up. He now runs *Amazon* as a floating restaurant. Wouldn't Arthur be proud – Joan certainly is.

Arthur would often chat about the Music Hall which had always interested him and some of the artistes he had seen or heard about. I was convinced that some of his technique had been influenced by the great radio and variety comedian Robb Wilton who was a master at making the audience feel he was always in charge, however ridiculous the situation. Arthur had also

his face and blow a sort of silent whistle. He could also create great comic effect from just a sniff and a look to acknowledge something that had been said, which either he could not be bothered to answer or did not know how to. Arthur had contradictory views about certain comic effects. He would say, 'I'm not doing that, it's pantomime stuff,' but in another scene he would do, for example, a perfectly legitimate comic fall and then embellish it by getting up with his cap askew and his glasses in a slanting position across his face, so the effect was as near to pantomime as it was possible to get.

I was touring in a play with Arthur and Joan in 1978 and I arranged a meeting between them and Sandy Powell and his wife Kay, both of whom I knew quite well. Arthur and Sandy admired each other's work and they spent a couple of hours over a few gin and tonics discussing this and that and making one another laugh. I've often wished I'd had a video camera with me that day, recording two masters of their craft in full sail.

During the tour of the play *Caught Napping*, Arthur was not sleeping well at night anyway, although he had the odd cat nap during the day and even sometimes on stage. So he got some sleeping tablets from his doctor. One evening he mistakenly did not take them until about seven in the morning with disastrous results. He was discovered sound asleep in his dressing-room just before curtain up and Joan and I tried to wake him by slapping his face, squirting a soda syphon on to the back of his neck and then even forcing his head out of the dressing-room window. Although he was half asleep, eventually we got him on stage to the top of the stairs where he had to make his entrance down a steep staircase. As the curtain went up, Arthur in the character of Potts the schoolmaster, dressed in shorts, tee-shirt and plimsoles, proceeded to descend the stairs. What followed next was unforgettable. He took a long time to reach the bottom step and on the way down went through the entire gambit of comic inventiveness. He may have been half asleep, but his natural talent for comedy, conjured up from the depths of a befuddled brain, soon had the audience laughing and applauding before a word had even been spoken.

Arthur's natural talent for comedy had, of course, been nurtured and refined over many years. In 1946 he began his acting career at the late age of thirty in repertory in Manchester. This was not only the start of his career but also a lifelong partnership with actress Joan Cooper. Joan takes up the story:

'Arthur was born in the very lovely village of Hayfield in Derbyshire. His father worked for the then London and North Eastern railway, and one of his duties was to arrange rail travel for touring theatrical companies. Arthur's early working life was spent with the Fairy Aviation Company before

A gala occasion. L to R: the Labour elder statesman Manny Shinwell, world boxing promoter, Jack Solomons and Arthur Lowe *(Joan Lowe)*

**Actress Joan
(Cooper) Lowe**
(Joan Lowe)

joining the Army prior to the 39-45 war. After a not too pleasant period in this country he was posted to the Middle East where he began to enjoy his service career in the Duke of Lancaster's Own Yeomanry. In fact with a little persuasion he might have made the Army his career.

He had a love of horses and became an expert horseman. It was while he was abroad in the Army that Arthur gained his first experience of 'theatre', although this was confined to delivering books of stage plays to outposts so that the troops could enjoy play-reading to relieve the boredom (which wasn't to last too long in the Middle East). He also enjoyed himself helping to organise troop shows while he was abroad. When he came home and was demobbed he broke the news to his parents that he didn't want to go back to Fairy Aviation, but wanted to try his luck in the theatre. His mum and dad were sympathetic to his wishes, at the same time probably thinking it was best he got it out of his system and once he'd tried it he would settle down again in a 'proper' job. His father gave him an introduction to Frank H. Fortescue who he knew, having done railway business with the impressario's touring theatrical companies. So it was that Arthur found himself on a cold January morning in 1946 at the Hulme Hippodrome, Manchester.

Flare Path was the first play of the new season at Hulme, and most of the company were old friends and had worked for Fortescue before. There was one person that nobody knew. He was wearing riding breeches and a heavy Army greatcoat. He was a very thin, short, slightly bald headed man, and obviously very cold. He said he'd just come back to England after four years in the Middle East. That day my whole life was changed. From then until Arthur's death in Birmingham during the run of *Home at Seven* in 1982 we were seldom apart.

At Hulme we did a new play every week, and two performances nightly, so Arthur got in a great amount of experience in a very short space of time. We talked from time to time over the next few weeks and he told me that his home was in Hayfield. That was our first bond because I was born in Chesterfield, so we were both Derbyshire people. We found we had many interests in common. My father was a cricket addict, so apparently was Arthur's. We had both been taken at a very early age to see some of the county matches at Chesterfield's ground. My dad was a church organist and choir master, and very dedicated to both, but occasionally cricket had to come first. I fell in love with Arthur during that season at Hulme, not perhaps the most romantic place to fall in love, and I think his parents were a little shocked at first; even though their son was now an actor, they looked upon stage people with a certain wariness. However, I got on famously with his parents and grew to adore his father. We were eventually married in 1948.

Arthur and Joan had come to London in 1946 as they both thought for Arthur's sake they should get into a repertory company within the London area. By 1950, after various short tours and a season at

Hereford, the daily rounds of the agents in London was beginning to pay off with several small film parts and radio broadcasts, including *Mrs Dale's Diary*. Those who have seen *Kind Hearts and Coronets*, which projected even further Alec Guinness' name, may have noticed the actor who played the reporter at the end of the film was Arthur Lowe. *Kind Hearts* was followed by another film, *The Spider and the Fly*, repertory again at Croydon and Bromley, and yet another film at Ealing Studios. In 1951 Arthur did his first television. At about this time he auditioned for *Call Me Madam* which Jack Hylton was presenting at the Coliseum. So he had arrived, as they say, in the West End, and in such a comparatively short time since that first season on the boards at Hulme Hippodrome.

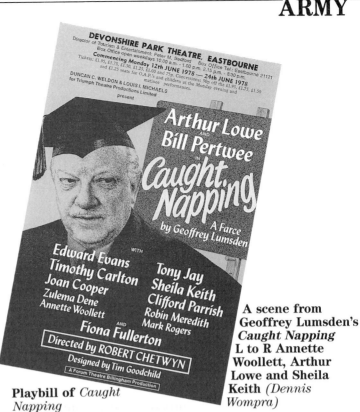

Playbill of *Caught Napping*

A scene from Geoffrey Lumsden's *Caught Napping* **L to R Annette Woollett, Arthur Lowe and Sheila Keith** *(Dennis Wompra)*

Joan Cooper, by now Mrs Lowe, takes up the story again:

'On more than one occasion, when Arthur Lowe and I were 'off duty' as it were, we were stopped by a young passer by with – 'Go on, Napoleon!' (Air Raid Warden Hodge's name for Mainwaring) 'Give him a black eye, and get your own back!'

6We found at this time our first real home together, a small flat in Rutland Gate. Almost at once I found myself pregnant, much to our delight. Arthur had been such a good stepfather to my son David by my previous and young marriage, it was wonderful that he was now going to have a son of his own. Film parts and radio followed, then the musical *Call Me Madam* and after that he went into another Jack Hylton production *Pal Joey* at the Princes, now renamed the Shaftesbury. More films, radio and television followed, and then he was back in the West End in 1955 in *The Pyjama Game* at the Coliseum.9

While Arthur was convalescing after an appendix operation, he began to drink wine rather than the occasional beer – nothing very expensive, about 2s (10p) a bottle. By the time I first met him he was quite a wine connoisseur. His son Stephen was growing up and already at kindergarten school and David was now at Hexham Grammer School near Joan's parents and had become proficient with his music studies, a talent inherited from Joan and her father. David is now Director of Music at Stowe School.

Soon after his operation, Arthur opened in London in *Dead Secret* with Paul Schofield. This certainly was Arthur's most important West End appearance to date. In 1960 he was offered a part in three episodes of a little series for Granada Television. He was to play Mr Swindley in *Coronation Street*. It was soon obvious that *Coronation Street* and Mr Swindley would continue, and this long-running series has, of course, become

a television phenomenon. Arthur suddenly found himself being recognised in public and, being a very shy person, was shocked and frightened. Even when *Dad's Army* was fairly well established, I have heard people call out to him 'How's Mr Swindley, then?'. He would stiffen up and quietly say, 'My name is Arthur Lowe.' Although it can be galling at times, actors have to remember that once they are on the 'box' regularly, they become public property. Why this should be so I do not know. Even now, after all these years, people will pass me in the street – and this applies to the other surviving members of the cast – and start singing 'Who do you think you are kidding Mr Hitler?', the show's signature tune. Arthur even used disguises and different voices in the hope that he would remain anonymous, but it didn't work. He was later given his own series by Granada called *Pardon the Expression* in which Mr Swindley was the main character. Arthur decided to call it a day with Mr Swindley in 1966 as he wished to move on to pastures new.

More theatre followed, then in 1967 Arthur was invited to lunch at the BBC by David Croft and Jimmy Perry. David Croft had produced many shows for the BBC and he and Jimmy wanted to talk to Arthur about a programme they were planning to write and which David would produce about the Home Guard. They wanted Arthur to play the central character of Captain Mainwaring. In civvy street he would be the manager of the local bank. Arthur returned home and discussed the proposition with Joan who undoubtedly had a great influence on Arthur's acceptance of the role. Joan always had good judgement and advice to offer on Arthur's various projects. After all,

Joan herself was an actress of long experience, have played a variety of roles in her career which began in 1939 working with the great Donald Wolfit, playing pages, ladies-in-waiting, and so on for 25s (£1.25p) a week on tour – and you had to pay your digs out of that and make sure you were always well dressed. Her later appearances were in J.B. Priestley's *Laburnham Grove* and *Beyond a Joke*, A.C. Sherriff's *Home at Seven* and *Caught Napping*, in which I was conscious of her acting ability as we had had several scenes together in that play. Joan was featured in several episodes of *Dad's Army* and in the stage version. But to get back to Arthur's original offer from the BBC.

As much as they liked the idea, I am sure that not even Arthur and Joan could have visualised at that point just what a huge success *Dad's Army* would eventually be. As Joan has said: 'The brilliant writing team of David Croft and Jimmy Perry gave us the happiest years of our life together. To be a part of that wonderful family of actors was a great delight.' It still amazes Joan, and it certainly does me, to look at Arthur's working diary and see just how much work he did prior to *Dad's Army* and during the run of the series. Most actors would have been satisfied with working in a popular television comedy series, Arthur did theatre, television and recording sessions for advertisements, voice-overs, reading children's stories and a radio series. He also managed to fit in more films, *Oh, Lucky Man* being one and the very funny *The Ruling Class* with Peter O'Toole in 1971 being another. The location for this film was a huge old country mansion not far from Nottingham. Arthur and Joan used to drive out for each day's filming with Jack

Preparing to film 'Sons of the Sea' on the Norfolk Broads. *(Bill Pertwee)*

Hawkins, one of the most admired and loved members of our profession. Although Joan also had a small part in the film she still had time to watch some cricket at the lovely Trent Bridge ground. Arthur and Joan grew very fond of Peter O'Toole during the filming of *The Ruling Class* and this applied to the crew with whom O'Toole used to play a primitive sort of cricket during the lunch-breaks. Joan told me:

❝This film occasioned the only anti-fan letter that I can remember Arthur receiving. He was playing a drunken Communist butler and had a wonderful scene shouting and swearing,

Arthur Lowe as a brilliant look-a-like Herbert Morrison, the Labour Cabinet Minister Arthur portrayed in the Granada Television production *Philby* (Joan Lowe)

Rehearsals of J.B. Priestley's *Laburnham Grove*. L to R: J.B. Priestley, Joan (Cooper) Lowe, Arthur Lowe *(Joan Lowe)*

breaking a family heirloom and generally being an absolute swine, before he was dragged off by the police. When the film was eventually released, an irate letter arrived from a lady saying that she had not expected to see such behaviour from 'Mr Swindley' or from 'Captain Mainwaring'. Arthur wrote back very politely, saying, 'Surely I am allowed to enjoy myself when covered by an X certificate.' You see, for once he had been able to forget his almost puritanical attitude to television and family entertainment. So Arthur really enjoyed making that film. **9**

He then portrayed Louis Pasteur in the medical drama *The Microbe Hunters*, most of which was filmed in Paris, and still more theatre at the Old Vic in *The Tempest* with Sir John Gielgud, proving again that Arthur was not just a fine comedy actor but a very good dramatic one too. Then from 1973 until 1977 *Dad's Army* took up most of his time with the radio version, stage musical, etc, which is described in more detail later. In 1977 he played Home Secretary Herbert Morrison, the Labour minister, in Granada's production of *Philby* the traitor. This was followed with a tour of Priestley's *Laburnham Grove*. In 1978 Arthur started a new series for BBC TV called *Potter*, who was a retired suburban busy-body, and a series for London Weekend TV called *Bless Me Father*. There was also a long theatre tour of *Caught Napping*. Then came the remake of the movie *The Lady Vanishes*, a spy thriller. Basil Redford and Naunton Wayne were the original cricket-loving Englishmen abroad caught up in a web of intrigue and espionage. Arthur played the Basil Redford part in the remake and Ian Carmichael the Naunton Wayne part. Arthur took Joan with him and they had a very happy time together seeing a lot of Austria and all the lovely film locations. Arthur came home to record more *Potter* and *Bless Me Father*, then had a season in a play at Shanklin on the Isle of Wight. Arthur and Joan moored the *Amazon* near Cowes and lived on her while they were there, which they greatly enjoyed. Working together and living on that lovely boat was heaven for them both, and the Isle of Wight is such a lovely place anyway. There was more to come, but not too much more. As Joan has said:

6In my quieter moments I

One of the happiest periods in Arthur Lowe's career. Ian Carmichael and Arthur Lowe relaxing in Austria where they were filming the remake of the 30's classic *The Lady Vanishes* (Joan Lowe)

naturally miss my dear Arthur, but I do thank the entertainment business for giving us so many happy moments together, particularly Paris when he was making *Pasteur*, Austria with *The Lady Vanishes*, and all those glorious days in Norfolk and Suffolk with our friends in *Dad's Army*.

Joan now lives in Arthur's late parents' cottage in the village of Hayfield. So you could say that she has come back to the source of a remarkable talent.

John Le Mesurier in relaxed mood. His portrayal of Sergeant Wilson provided the perfect foil for Arthur Lowe as Captain Mainwaring.
(Peter Way)

'Being in *Dad's Army* was like belonging to a gentleman's club.' – John Le Mesurier

John Le Mesurier

If anyone had told me before *Dad's Army* that a close friendship would develop between John Le Mesurier and myself over the years I would have been very surprised, as we were both so different in upbringing and theatrical background, but that is exactly what happened. In the lunch-break during the first day's rehearsal for the programme at the Feathers Pub off the Hogarth roundabout at Chiswick, John came over to me and said, 'I'd like to buy you a drink.' And that was the first of many noggins we would share together during a long association. You see, John's career had encompassed many, many films, in which he had worked with some of the big names in our business and he was on first name terms with practically all of them. He would quote people by their Christian names without any effect or desire to impress: 'I had a lovely week or two with Fred [Astaire] in Rome' or 'Noel [Coward] once said to me when we had a day together ...', and 'David [Niven] and I had a lot of laughs when he was over here last ...' I have to admit that it did impress me and certainly made me feel that here was someone who had certainly been around and, I felt sure, would have many interesting stories to relate. My only counter to the list of international film and stage actors that he had known and worked with was to tell him about a summer show I had done on the pier at Brighton, or about some rather dodgy weeks in variety that I had endured at West Bromwich or Cleethorpes. Our musical tastes were in one or two respects similar, but John was far more familiar with most types from jazz to light opera, than I could ever be.

Against this background it may seem surprising that we became such good mates, but there were a number of reasons why it happened. First, we made each other laugh. Just as I enjoyed his slightly sophisticated humour, he liked my far more earthy approach. John had tremendous admiration for music hall and circus folk. His lovely and vivacious wife Joan came from a circus and funfair background, so his rapport with the circus came naturally to John. He used to say that circus people had heart, and that meant a lot to him. I have some roots in the music hall and know a few stories about the greats of that profession, and I used to tell him anecdotes about Harry Tate, the eccentric comedian who worked in the earlier part of this century, and Robb Wilton and Jimmy James. John would say: 'Tell me that story about Harry Tate again' and I could hear his familiar chuckle even before I had finished. I used to go back to John's flat in Kensington for the occasional night after a long day in the studio, and we would sit up until the early hours chatting about some of life's eccentrics – he was rather fond of eccentrics. That slightly absent-minded attitude of his was not put on, particularly when it came to mundane things like food or organising his mail. If, however, a correspondent interested him, he would reply promptly and at length. His wife Joan looked after the house they had in Ramsgate and where her parents also lived, and she would come up to London once or twice a week and have a good cooking session, putting all sorts of dishes into the freezer for John. One night I remember he went to the freezer and took out something that he fancied to eat, but it was at the bottom of the pile so he had to take out the other items first. When I got up in the morning all these items were still on the kitchen table, completely defrosted and therefore ruined for future use.

After a long recording session one day at Television Centre when Ian Lavender and I had been up to the waist in a water-tank for hours on end, I had to drive up to Stamford where I was to compere a series of concerts at a caravan rally. It was pouring with rain when I got into the car at about 10.30pm ready to start the long journey North. John appeared at the car window and said, 'Where are you off to, Billy?' (he always called me Billy). 'I'm off to Stamford for the weekend', I told him and explained the reason why. He asked if he could come with me as he was not doing any-

thing for the weekend. I replied 'Well, O.K.' He then said 'If we could pop round to the flat on the way, I'll get my toothbrush'. We headed North with a rainstorm so fierce that I lost a windscreen wiper. Half-way up the A1 we both felt a bit peckish so we pulled up at a Carman's Café – there were many of these dotted about the country at that time. Unfortunately, or fortunately, whichever way you look at it, nearly all have been replaced

Joan and John Le Mesurier at home in Ramsgate. *(Joan Le Mesurier)*

by neon-lit service centres, but how welcome those little 'caffs' were to weary theatricals on their journeys up and down the country. On that particular night, John and I tucked into bacon, egg, sausage, baked beans and fried bread with a doorstep slice of fresh white bread, and all washed down with a cup of steaming Camp coffee, black liquid which was poured out of a bottle. I think Camp coffee lost some of its appeal when the word 'camp' became general theatrical jargon for someone who was a bit eccentric or OTT (over the top). We were both recognised in the café that night and John conversed as comfortably with the various lorry drivers who came up to him as he would have done with society folk at The Ritz. He used to say, 'As long as a person is interesting he deserves one's attention.' He really did not have much time for bores and, after putting up with some ridiculous conversation, would say quietly, 'That fellow invented boredom.'

But back to our trip to Stamford on that wet night. I was being put up at the Haycock Inn at Wansford. When we arrived at about 1am we were told that they were full up (mostly with caravan rally organisers – they were no fools, they were not going to spend a weekend in a caravan in a wet field!). I was told

there were two beds in the room that had been booked for me and that was the best they could do. John said 'I'm quite happy to sleep with Billy.' The receptionist gave us a funny look, but I was too tired to allay her fears about 'those theatrical people'. I was just hoping John would omit to mention the Camp coffee we had on the way up. We had a sandwich and a large Scotch sent up to the room. I dropped off to sleep straight away, which was not surprising as not only had I spent the day in a water-tank but I had also had a rotten drive up the A1, normally a road I enjoy driving on. At four o'clock in the morning, I woke up to find the light on, the window open, and John sitting up in bed writing.

'What the devil's going on?' I asked. 'It's four in the morning'. John replied 'I'm writing some words to accompany that dreadful noise you've

John Le Mesurier getting a 'touch-up' from the make-up girls. (*Bill Pertwee*)

been making.' Apparently, the eggs, bacon, sausage, fried bread, baked beans, Camp coffee, late-night sandwich and the Scotch had all been too much for my digestive system and in my sleep I'd had a touch of the wind, to say the least!

I repeated this story at dear John's funeral and memorial service in London at the suggestion of Joan. I must say it brought much laughter from the congregation on both occasions, and I'm sure John wouldn't have minded. In fact, I could almost hear him saying, 'Oh Billy, do be quiet', accompanied by that quiet and infectious chuckle.

But to return to the rest of that weekend with the caravan club. When we reached the site in the morning, the previous evening's storm had all but wrecked the two huge marquees that had been erected for the concerts. The site held something like a thousand caravans. John took his coat off and, together with all the many willing hands, got down to banging in the steel pegs, hooking up the guy ropes and generally making himself useful. Once this was done, still covered in mud but obviously enjoying himself, John seemed to be invited into every caravan on the site.

John never did things by halves. He drove a not-too-new Ford car and one morning on the way to rehearsals he decided that he had had enough and didn't need a car any more, particularly in London, so he left it there and then under the Hammersmith flyover, and although he had had a licence since a very early age, he never owned another car.

Some days John would arrive at the studios looking a little tired. We would ask him if he had had a bad night and he would reply, 'No, on the contrary, a most pleasant one. I went to Ronnie Scott's Club and was so enjoying the music and meeting friends I didn't realise it was as late as it was and I didn't get home until 4am.' But late nights certainly didn't affect John's ability to learn his lines for he was always very quick at getting the words firmly in his head very early on in rehearsal. He was a great jazz fan and knew people like Humphrey Lyttleton, Johnny Dankworth and Cleo Laine, Nat Gonella, and Ronnie Scott of course, and many more. I'm sure John would have enjoyed Clint Eastwood's movie tribute to saxaphonist Charlie Parker, had he lived to see it.

When John and I drove up to filming sessions at Thetford, we avoided going via the A11 from London. We used to go up the A1 and then cut off through Royston and join the A11 later. We would stop at a small old-fashioned but extremely pleasant hotel for a drink and bite to eat. This would bring memories of the 1930s flooding back to John. He used to attend various balls at the hotel, anniversaries, birthdays, etc, and those summer balls were held in the grounds of the hotel in marquees (he seems to have an affinity with marquees) where the young set would dance the night away to the music of Ambrose or Roy Fox and their bands.

On another occasion when we were going up for the annual filming at Thetford, I asked John what time he wanted me to pick him up. At the most, even with a stop for refreshment, we could do it comfortably in four hours. On this occasion we weren't needed in Thetford until Sunday night, so I thought tea-time on Sunday would be a good time to leave London. Much to my surprise, John asked if we could go up on Friday so that we could stop off in Newmarket and go to the national stud, have a look

'Do you think that's wise sir?'

round, and also go and see a few trainers. John was on fairly intimate terms with some of the racing fraternity and was a real horse-lover and frequent visitor to race-tracks around the country when he had time. I agreed to go up on the Friday and, after a day in Newmarket, we then went on to stay at the Angel Hotel at Bury St Edmunds. This was John's home town where his father had had a most successful law business, and that evening in Bury, John and I

'What's to become of us all?' John Le Mesurier waiting to film on the Britannia Pier, Great Yarmouth: 'Menace from the Deep' *(Bill Pertwee)*

waitress came in for it during that dinner at the Angel. She was quite elderly and when she was serving the soup John suddenly said to her in a rather loud voice, 'What about bloody Billingham!' The waitress practically threw the soup at us and ran for her life. A different waitress came to take our order for the main course. The whole Billingham saga will unfold later.

When we arrived in Thetford on that Sunday night after our two-day journey (which nor-

visited practically every pub in the place before we headed back to the Angel for a late supper. At that point John was rather concerned about the stage version of *Dad's Army* that we were about to embark upon later in the summer. We were going to open in Billingham, Cleveland, before coming into the West End and few of us had heard of Billingham. John kept asking, 'Why do we have to go to this Billingham Place, Billy? It's miles from anywhere, we shall probably all get lost.' Even the

mally took three or four hours), Arthur Lowe asked John what sort of journey we had had, and John replied, 'Fine, it took two days.' Arthur gave us that famous look of his and just said 'Extraordinary' and walked away. I explained to Arthur that we had spent some time in Newmarket and he said 'Oh yes, he pats horses, you know.'

Having been born in Bury St Edmunds, John quite naturally had a long affinity with the countryside, although he lived in London for most of his

adult life. He loved horses and dogs, old pubs with their local characters and village greens, preferably with a cricket match in progress. He had played cricket, in fact, for Suffolk and was probably up to county standard in his young days. His cricketing prowess was nurtured at Sherborne School. John was fascinated by the theatre in his teens when he used to come up to London, and was rather jealous of what he thought must be a terribly glamorous life. After he became an actor, he was well aware of the hard work behind the business at acting. In fact, he often said to me, 'It's not easy work, is it?'

John was twenty-three before he suddenly decided that he wanted to go into the theatre. Up to that time he was intent on following his father into the family law business and was in the process of travelling on his father's behalf when he decided that the legal profession wasn't for him. The urge to become an actor overtook him when he was travelling on a train from Waterloo and as he passed Sandown Park race-course (racing and its environment seemed to punctuate his life) the decision was finalised in his mind. The fact that the day before he had been to see Fred and Adèle Astaire in *Funny Face* at the Princes Theatre probably had something to do with it. At that time, of course, he could not have imagined that one day he would work with the great Fred Astaire. Having had a fairly easy and comfortable upbringing, it must have been something of a shock when he went into repertory earning just £4 or £5 a week.

In his highly amusing autobiography *A Jobbing Actor*, John recalls his first London engagement as 'understudy' in *Gaslight* at the Apollo Theatre. He did, however, take over one of the leading roles when the

John Le Mesurier/ Sergeant Wilson as Wellington (centre) in Mainwaring's nightmare in 'A Soldier's Farewell'. *(Bill Pertwee)*

play went on tour. At this time John had met and married a young female impresario, June Melville. A female impresario was something of a pheno-menon among a male-orientated business, but a pretty one was even more rare. He continued touring and June Melville continued with her job. Then came the war, September 1939.

That was the start of a change of life, not just for John but for many people. He became an air raid warden in Chelsea, but there was still some touring to do. Returning with June one day, they found their house in Smith Square, Chelsea, rased to the ground by a German bomb. After this John was called up and went to do his bit for his country, but it appears that some of the military personnel had doubts

as to his enthusiasm for life in the army. The answer was found by recommending him for a commission. He was posted aboard and spent much of his time in India. When he returned for demob and civvy street, his marriage to June, like so many other marriages of that period, became a war casualty

John returned to touring with the theatre, but his sights were set on films, and before long the round of agents paid off. In 1947 John was taken by a friend to the famous Players' Theatre Victorian music hall under the arches at Charing Cross. It was the first of many visits and there he met actress Hattie Jaques who eventually became his second wife. Hattie was soon climbing the ladder through Tommy Handley's radio series *ITMA* and later in *Educating Archie*.

John's film career was also prospering and eventually he became one of the best known faces on the silver screen with *Private's Progress, Brothers-in-*

Mainwaring: 'Never mind patting it Wilson, just get up on it. My platoon is going to be a mobile platoon.' Arthur Lowe/Mainwaring; John Le Mesurier/ Wilson; Clive Dunn/Jones and John Laurie/Fraser in 'Man of the Hour' (BBC)

Law, I'm Alright Jack, and many others. The British film industry was in full swing and John, together with other actors like Richard Attenborough, Jack Hawkins, Peter Sellers, Norman Wisdom, Donald Sinden and all the J Arthur Rank starlets, were becoming national names. Hattie Jaques, too, was making her way in films which led her to long association with the *Carry On* company and eventually into the enormously popular television series with Eric Sykes. They had started a family and the two boys, Robin and Kim, were now growing up. They would eventually enter the competitive world of pop music, and make it, very successfully.

Unfortunately, John and Hattie's marriage ran into troubled waters, through no one's fault in particular, and they parted. They were still fond of one another and used to spend time together. Sunday lunch was almost a must if they were both free and everyone remained on the best of terms, even after John had married Joan. He was terribly upset when Hattie died and always remembered her with tremendous affection. I only met Hattie on a couple of occasions, once when I worked on a television episode with her, and found her to be a most charming and gracious lady.

By 1965 John had married Joan Malin. Her parents were from the fairground business and on our once and only meeting I found them delightful, perhaps quieter than their daughter, who I liked immediately when John first introduced us. John was not always the easiest person to handle, but Joan was generally quick to sense the reason and find a solution. Any mood that he got into was usually the result of being bored and nothing else. He was the sort of chap who could quite hap-pily board a plane for Hong Kong at a moment's notice for a few days' filming, armed only with a toothbrush and razor. The thought of a long run in the theatre was obviously a depressing one in his later years. Mind you it does the same to a lot of actors. It says a great deal about his marriage to Joan that they overcame certain difficulties and yet still remained sweethearts until he died. Shortly before his death, John stayed with us for a few weeks while he was doing a play, and he would phone Joany, as he called her, nearly every night. We loved having him to stay with us. He used to have breakfast in the garden and our dog Biffa would sit at his feet as it they had been chums for years.

During the *Dad's Army* era, John worked on many other projects – as did other members of the cast – voice-overs by the dozen, other series and the television play called *The Traitor,* for which he won an award as Best Actor. I know that meant an awful lot to him. Just before the last series of *Dad's Army* , John went on a theatre tour aboard and was taken ill. He recovered from that, but it had taken its toll and when we arrived at Thetford for the filming session of that last series, we were all told beforehand not to show surprise at his thin and strained appearance. Even though we had been warned, it still came as a shock when we met up that evening at the Bell Hotel. A few days in East Anglia, however, back among the 'boys', soon had him somewhere near his amusing and convivial self. So it was still a shock to all of us when he finally, in his own words, 'conked out'. He'd certainly given me many laughs during a nine-year friendship and he hadn't finish then. There were even one or two surprises at his funeral.

> John Le Mesurier had a favourite saying when a situation got a bit fraught or he was not happy with his surroundings. He would say 'This is like a tiny peep into hell'.

Clive Dunn, OBE

How can you accurately describe someone like Clive Dunn? Clown, actor, trick cyclist, dancer, raconteur, *Top of the Pops* chart topper and accomplished artist who is good enough to have his work exhibited.

Clive's experience goes back a long way. He comes from a theatrical family, and a very successful one at that. His grandfather was music hall comedian Frank Lynn, who wrote and performed his own comic songs. Clive's mother was Connie Clive, a comedienne of some note, and his father was Bobby Dunn, singer and raconteur. This family

'Don't panic! Don't panic!'

Clive Dunn who played Corporal Jones, a key member of the Home Guard and the local butcher. Jones's van provided the transport for the platoon and had a vital part in several hilarious adventures. Corporal Jones's catch-phrase 'Don't panic! Don't panic!' was known throughout Britain. *(David Croft)*

background of making people laugh influenced Clive at an early age, and his portrayal of dotty old gents on stage and television had the hallmark of music hall about them. Without that unique background I do not think any other actor could have been as inventive with those characters as Clive was. Not that he isn't a good actor, but that very useful mix of music hall and revue in his family background helped him, particularly when the script-writers supplied some great situations to work with, which certainly happened to Clive as far as *Dad's Army* was concerned.

Before tackling any comedy business or routine, Clive is often hesitant and gives the impression that he is not very enthusiastic at the prospect of doing it. After a while it is obvious that this diffidence is because he wants time to think about what he is going to do and how to get the best results. When I first worked with him I really thought he was being rather off-hand with the writers and his fellow actors, but I soon realised that this was how he worked. The nervous laughter that accompanied his assessment of a situation was used as a cover for his hesitancy, a way of keeping the ball in the air, as he didn't want to isolate himself completely from the situation and those associated with it. Any other actor might have walked away and said first, 'Well, I'll think about it.' His genuine laughter and good humour at all other times was very infectious.

There is a story about Clive's Uncle Gordon and the salmon and cucumber sandwiches at Ascot races in his autobiography *Permission to Speak*. He related this story to me one day during rehearsals and he had me rolling about with laughter. I have always found him great company and look forward to meeting up with him again, which is not so

Corporal Jones: 'Here come them Jerry bombers again. I hope they don't hit my shop, I've just had a delivery of offal! *(Columbia Pictures Industries Inc.)*

often nowadays because he lives much of the time in Portugal where he and his family, wife Priscilla and daughters Polly and Jessica, have a restaurant. Clive has always been interested in food, so it must be a great restaurant with that family presiding. At whatever time of day you dropped into the Dunn household in their then London home at Barnes there always seemed to be something to eat. Grapes, biscuits, cheese, some sort of cake he had seen in the local delicatessen, and certainly a bottle of wine. One got the impression that the whole household was run like a continental family home – with anybody welcome at any time. Connie, Clive's mother, lived in the house next door and was very independent and as lively as a cricket, despite her age. Clive and Cilla and the girls were always very conscious of her welfare and you would generally hear a chorus of voices ringing out at odd times, 'Anyone been up to see Connie this morning?'. I used to talk to Connie about the Fol-de-Rols (I have a nice postcard of her in one of the company groups), as I had also been a 'Fol' and we both knew the amazing governor of that show, Rex Newman, although Connie's friendship with him started many years before I was in the company. Rex not only owned the best concert party, The Fol-de-Rols, which conquered almost every seaside town and many inland ones as well in the country, but in his time he was responsible for writing a lot of material for the original Crazy Gang. He also wrote a very successful 1930s musical entitled *Mr Cinders* which was revived a few years ago in London, once again to critical acclaim.

When Clive and Cilla started to put down roots in Portugal it didn't surprise me. They had both been regular visitors for years and the continental style of mixing together family and friends and different artistic talents, which they had always encouraged, in the atmosphere of a small community will give them a lot of pleasure. No doubt the Dunn home is strewn with delicacies just waiting for the first caller of the day to arrive. I have promised I will go out and spend a week or two with them at a later date. I know they'll give the 'Peruvian Inca' (as they call me) a wonderful time. I don't speak Portuguese but my mother did. Being Brazilian it was her first language. So where did the Inca originate? My great-grandmother was one.

Coincidence is a strange thing. One day in the very early Seventies I told Clive that my family and I were moving from the coast and coming nearer to London, in fact to Surrey. I described the area and Clive told me he used to visit a composer friend 'down that way'. He started to describe the house and within minutes I knew it was the one I had just bought. And would you believe, it came to light that the composer's wife was the choreographer for a big Blackpool summer show that my wife Marion had been in when she was a professional dancer. Even more coincidences followed on from this, but let's get back to Clive Dunn.

It was obvious that he would go into 'the business'. His father was not keen on his following a theatrical career but eventually helped him. Almost his first job was as a boy extra in a Will Hay film *Boys Will Be Boys*, but being good theatrical parents Connie and Bobby decided that Clive should attend a stage school and they enrolled him at one of the very best, Italia Conti. With Italia Conti you had a chance to work in some professional seasonal shows

Opposite: **Clive Dunn.**
(Ceristone Photography)

In the event of observing German parachutists landing, telephone High Wycombe 26.

Standing Orders of 4th Battalion, Buckinghamshire LDV, Summer 1940.

which was wonderful experience. Clive was involved in some of these, and then went out into the hazardous world of commercial repertory, stage managing and playing small parts, and, as was fairly usual at that time, experiencing the management saying 'Sorry lads and lasses, the tour finishes on Saturday, the public aren't coming in.' Then would start the problem of paying off the landlady and finding the fare to get home, and waiting for the next engagement to come along.

Soon after this, Clive's 'next engagement' was in the Second World War, and his experience was far more traumatic than that of a tour closing after a few weeks. He was taken prisoner by the Germans in Greece, and although there is a humorous undercurrent to these extraordinary years in captivity, as he recalls

in his autobiography, it is obvious that only a fit person with a good sense of humour could have survived them. Other people were going through hell in the Far East or in German concentration camps, but certainly Clive's recollection of the horrendous events in his life as a prisoner make them both compulsive and humorous reading.

Clive has been described as a pro's comic actor, and I wouldn't disagree with this and I don't think he would either. In the medium of television, or the Players' Theatre, for instance, where he played on and off for many years, Clive would invent strange characters and originate offbeat dialogue. If this were done in the big variety theatre, a throw-away line or quiet aside would have no value. So one might say he was created for the small screen, which

Clive Dunn in close up in the tree. *(BBC)*

Clive Dunn/Corporal Jones disguised as a tree trying to capture an enemy windmill in 'Don't Forget the Diver' *(BBC)*

eventually came his way in great abundance with programmes like *Bootsie and Snudge*, *It's a Square World* and various other projects, together with all the many comic lunatics who have brightened our lives over the years.

It was at about this time that he met actress Priscilla Morgan, who was to become his second wife. Priscilla was already a well-established actress, having had major roles in radio and television plays, and was at that time with the Royal Shakespeare Company at Stratford-on-Avon alongside such famous actors as Albert Finney, Paul Robeson and Charles Laughton, and now she found herself being chased around by a panto-mimist disguised as various old men. It must have been Clive's sense of humour that appealed to her, for Cilla tele-phoned her mother one day and said 'Mummy, I'm going to marry a middle-aged comed-ian.' So Clive in his most athletic style 'had her up the aisle', as they say, quick as a flash.

When *Dad's Army* began, and although I didn't know Clive until then, I realised that he had a lot of artistic talent, and that he knew how to enjoy it. He and John Le Mesurier were already old buddies and, because of my concert party and my variety connections, which Clive was in tune with because of his and his parents' earlier work in that direction, the three of us soon had some topics in common.

Clive certainly had a talent for picking the right material when he picked the song 'Grandad' to record. This really was an extraordinary event, not just in Clive's life but for his family and those close to him or associated with him, as we, the cast of *Dad's Army*, were at that time. During the week or two before the record's release Clive seemed to be certain that it would be fairly successful. I heard it one afternoon at about this time in John Le Mesurier's flat in Baron's court and we liked it. It was simple and it had a good hook line (those repeating phrases that are easy for the public to pick up), but I don't think anyone realised what an impact it was going to make. Once it was released first one disc jockey started playing it, then others followed suit and before long it was being played regularly. Now came the crunch. Clive

was immediately caught up in the publicity machine that only the record business knows how to use. Clive was being rushed around the coun-try on promotional trips. There were television appear-ances. Managements wanted him for theatre shows and contracts were being drawn up for this, that and the other. It was amazing that he coped with it all. There was also the fact that *Dad's Army* was beginning to take off in a big way, and now he had a num-ber one hit record and appearances on *Top of the Pops* to make. His family were very supportive, of course, and also very proud of Dad – well, who wouldn't be? From an extra in a Will Hay film to *Top of the Pops* was quite something.

Clive is always good com-pany on social occasions. In 1988 several of us went to a restaurant after appearing on the *Wogan* show and Clive was about to order a couple of dishes of slightly Mediter-ranean origin when I said 'You don't want that, you can have that in Portugal, have so and so.' Eventually he did order all the things I had suggested, but after playing with the food for a bit he said, 'I don't like any of that.' Someone enquired as to why he had ordered it and Clive replied 'The Peruvian made me have it.' After several bottles of wine and much reminiscing about old times, we were ready for home and seeing Clive off to the airport for the return trip to Portugal. As he left, he said to the head waiter, 'I've really enjoyed myself, but don't ever employ my friend as a chef – he'll empty the place.' No doubt Clive will get his own back on me when I visit him in Portu-gal where he and his family now run the Café Royale in Quarteira, and if any of you dear readers visit the Royale have one for me!

> A woman talking to her friend one evening said 'One thing about the bombing, it takes your mind off the blackout'.

Arnold Ridley, OBE

Anyone who writes thirty-five plays in long hand, including one blockbuster, is entitled to have writer's cramp, but when the diagnosis of loss of use of your arm and hand reveals that the nerve on the inside of that arm has died, it really is a serious business and would have made most people feel like giving up any hope of ever working again. Arnold Ridley, however, the gentle Private Godfrey of *Dad's Army*, was an exception, for beneath the surface he was a very strong and determined man.

Educated in his home town of Bath and nearby Bristol University it was thought that Arnold would become a schoolteacher, but in 1914 he joined the Theatre Royal, Bristol, to take up an acting career. Later that same year he enlisted in the Somerset Light Infantry and this led him into World War I and the bloody fighting in France. Arnold was eventually invalided out in 1917, his left hand and fingers badly injured, his body pitted with shrapnel, and suffering from a blow on the head from the rifle butt of a German soldier that was later to affect him with serious blackouts.

Arnold's life was equal to any adventure story. He wasn't sure what to do when he came out of the army, but decided to continue where he had left off before the war and was taken on by the Birmingham Repertory Company and later the Plymouth company, but was forced to give up acting in 1921 because of the severe injuries he had received in France. A very despondent Arnold went home to Bath and worked in his father's bootshop. He had been a fine sportsman in his young days, playing high-grade cricket and Rugby for Bath. So apart from the pain and discomfort he was suffering in 1921, his frustration at having to give up his sporting activities and the problem of not being able to work properly must have been very depressing indeed. He later became the secretary of Bath Football Club and held that position for seventeen years, when he became the club's president. He was eventually made a life member. When I knew him he was always anxious to find out the latest cricket and rugby scores and particularly those of Bath Football Club.

In the early Twenties Arnold didn't know whether he would ever act again, and it was while he was working for his father that he wrote his first play. He took this to a theatrical producer in London and although it was received with some enthusiasm, unfortunately the producer had some other important business to attend to (they always have) and could not take the project any further at that time. Arnold was desperately disappointed and after the meeting went to a theatre to

Arnold Ridley took on the role of the gentle Private Godfrey, always needing to 'be excused'. *(John Vere Brown)*

see a thriller. He thought it was very ineffectual and was convinced he could write a better one. Not long after this he was travelling by rail from the Midlands back to his home in Bath and he had to change at a country station, Mangotsfield Junction, where he had a four-hour wait. While he was sitting on the deserted platform the idea came to him for another play. The slightly eerie atmosphere of the empty station and a fairy tale theme that he remembered sparked off the idea for *The Ghost Train*. He wrote the outline of it in about a week in his father's shop at night and decided to complete it and offer it to a management. As a play it was not easy to produce technically. Although some very spectacular musicals had been mounted in London, it was a daring piece for a play. *The Ghost Train* was first produced at Brighton, but

was not a success. It was shelved for a while, then a tour was arranged, the result of which still did not give any real indication of the eventual success that was to come its way worldwide. After the tour it was produced at the St Martin's Theatre in London in 1925 and accompanied by a clever advertising campaign. It became a West End hit and ran for over six hundred performances there. Later it transferred to the Garrick and then the Comedy Theatre. It just goes to prove that some managements who have faith in a product are prepared to gamble on their intuition even after, as was the case with *The Ghost Train*, it had had two unsuccessful attempts in the provinces. Suddenly Arnold was in the money and experiencing some notoriety as a West End author. He almost immediately wrote another play called *The Wrecker* in collaboration with another writer. Although some people thought it was even better than *The Ghost Train* and although it was produced at the New Theatre, it was not a hit.

During the rest of the Twenties and early Thirties Arnold was a prolific playwright with London productions that included *Third Time Lucky, Easy Money, Beggar My Neighbour* – all three of which were also filmed – *Glory Be, The Keepers of Youth* and *Tabitha*. Arnold adapted *Peril at End House* for the stage from an Agatha Christie thriller and certainly would have collaborated with her on future occasions had it not been for World War II, because he immediately struck up a rapport and friendship with Agatha Christie on their first meeting.

In 1935 he founded his own film company and with a partner and the backing of a bank, went to work on their first production *Royal Eagle*. When

Actor Arnold Ridley was also a playwright with 35 plays to his credit. *(Althea Ridley)*

the film was previewed it got marvellous notices, but half-way through their second movie the bank went bust. Arnold was left in serious financial difficulty, but rather than declaring himself bank-rupt, he paid off all his creditors personally. It took him nearly twenty years to achieve this, but every penny was paid back. He enlisted in the Army in 1939 and was sent to France with the rank of major. He became severely shell-shocked during the evacuation from France in 1940 and was reprimanded when he returned to England for failing to inform the authorities of his World War I wounds. He was invalided out of the Army and decided to join ENSA (The Entertainment National Service Association). ENSA were sending com-panies of entertainers all over the British Isles and to His Majesty's ships in home waters. Some of these compan-ies were made up of just two or three artistes working from the back of a lorry or even solo performers at a lonely gun site. Other productions were much bigger when facilit-ies allowed and Arnold's first assignment was to direct his own play *The Ghost Train* for a national tour.

Auditions for the play were held at Drury Lane Theatre in London, the headquarters of ENSA, and one morning a lady arrived at the theatre to read for one of the parts and was greeted by a small gentleman with a funny old hat who led her on to the stage. The lady thought the gentleman was the stage door-keeper, but was very soon to find out that he was, in fact, the author and director of the play. The act-ress was Althea Parker who had come to ENSA after driv-ing ambulances at night during the blitz on London. Althea had heard about Arnold from a friend a couple of years previously and said,

'He sounds the sort of man I'd like to marry.' At Drury Lane, after she had got used to his funny hat, she accepted an invitation from Arnold to have a drink and decided then and there that she would marry him, and this they eventually did, but not until the war finished. Meantime, they toured in plays together and they also did a season at the Malvern Festival.

Arnold Ridley on location in Norfolk.
(David Croft)

Althea Parker had gone with her family to New Zealand when she was a very young girl and had done her initial stage-work in that country. She returned to England in 1937 and immediately got a job in the Tyrone Guthrie Company at the Old Vic acting alongside such distinguished actors and actresses as John Mills, Vivienne Leigh and Ralph Richardson. Althea was later chosen to appear in J.B. Priestley's *Time and The Conways*. After she and Arnold were married and their son Nick was born in 1947, Althea did little stage-work but some prestigious television plays.

By this time Arnold had decided to concentrate on an acting career. He loved being a father, although he had always

Arnold Ridley, with his wife, actress Althea Parker *(Althea Ridley)*

given the impression that he wasn't too keen on having children around. Many years later he and Nick were having a chat and his son said, 'I expect I was a mistake.' Althea replied, 'You certainly weren't, I planned it,' and I'm sure she had. Nick's affection for his father was not isolated as far as children are concerned. During the run of Dad's Army it was very apparent who the

young children would go to first when they were collecting autographs. Arnold's mailbag was always full of letters from children, which is not surprising, for 'little ones' have an instinct as to who is their 'friend'.

In about 1952 it became impossible for Arnold to use his right arm and hand because the nerve had died. This had almost certainly been caused by his lengthy period of writing which he always initially did in long hand. It was decided to operate and take the nerve from the back of the arm and graft it on to the inside – an operation that had been performed only once before and not very successfully. However, Arnold went ahead with it and fortunately it proved worthwhile. While he was recovering from the surgery, Emile Littler – the well-known impresario, let it be known that he wished to stage a musical version of *The Ghost Train* at the Palace Theatre to be entitled *Happy Holiday*, but on condition that Arnold should make over to him half the rights of the play for ever. This Arnold agreed to, but the musical was not a success. However, Arnold never regretted his decision to allow Littler to control half the rights of *The Ghost Train* because from that time, the impresario collected the royalties in a very business-like way, which other managements in the past had certainly not done. That little idea of a train story that came into Arnold's mind on a deserted railway station in the 1920s had certainly become a money-spinner. Apart from the many productions of it all over the world, it was also made into three films, including a silent version, a second sound version starring Jack Hulbert and Cicely Courtneidge, and a third one featuring Arthur Askey and Richard Murdoch in the 1940s.

During the Sixties and Seventies Arnold featured in radio's long running series *The Archers*. He also appeared several times in *Coronation Street* and was a regular in *Crossroads*, playing the vicar. As with John Laurie, *Dad's Army* opened up yet another phase in Arnold's career when

Mainwaring: 'This is not a concert party you know Godfrey, this is war. You look ridiculous dressed up in a pierrot costume. We're supposed to be camouflaged for snow manoeuvres.'
L to R foreground: Arnold Ridley as Godfrey and Arthur Lowe as Mainwaring in 'Love of Three Oranges' *(BBC)*

'May I be excused?

he was already into his seventies. It was amazing to watch him picking up the laughs in the series with his quiet underplaying of the character Godfrey. In between various productions of the series he also did some more stagework including a long tour with Phil Silvers (Sergeant Bilko) in *A Funny Thing Happened on the Way to the Forum*, and a sell-out season at the Yvonne Arnaud Theatre, Guildford, playing the porter in *The Ghost Train*. I saw this production and Arnold was marvellous, as was the play which I was seeing for the first time. It was also produced at a later date at the Old Vic but, in Arnold's words, 'it was not a memorable production'.

Arnold always seemed to me to be a disciplined person. He was punctual at rehearsals and learnt his lines and moves very quickly. During the whole run of the series I saw him cross only once and he had reason to be on that occasion.

He had a little chuckle if he enjoyed hearing a joke or while telling some anecdote himself. He had the look of a cheeky schoolboy at times. Midway through one afternoon, when we were filming out in the country, he told David Croft that he wasn't feeling too well. David immediately summoned a unit car and told Arnold to go back to the hotel and rest. When we arrived back much later we saw Arnold walking out of a nearby pub. We said, 'You should be resting,' and he replied, 'Well, I had a gin in the hotel and felt so much better I thought I'd go out and have another one.' This was followed by that chuckle and twinkle of the eye.

In 1976 he was the subject of *This Is Your Life*. The idea of surprising him was that we were going to do a rehearsal for a scene at Marylebone Station and he was told, as we all were, to report to the station in the afternoon. Naturally, we were all in on the secret and so was Althea – in fact, she had known for several months but had kept it to herself, which is not always easy when you are with somebody every day as is the case with husband and wife. At the appropriate time Althea was hiding in the ticket inspector's office with Eamonn Andrews and once we were all lined up in front of the cameras, which had to be disguised as BBC equipment, Eamonn, in the uniform of station master, introduced himself to Arnold and produced the 'red book'. He certainly was stunned, and all he said was 'Does my wife know about this?'. It was certainly a relief to Althea when it all fitted into place. We were all whisked off to the studio ready to record the programme which included not only many theatrical friends and family, but also a lot of his contemporaries from Bath Rugby Club.

In 1982 to the delight of everyone who knew him, Arnold was awarded the OBE in the New Year's honours list for services to the theatre. By this time, failing health was overtaking him and he was confined more and more to the flat, but was cared for in a very loving and sympathetic way by Althea. She had been a great support and strength during their whole married life in a way that perhaps only a person connected with the theatre's ups and downs, of which Arnold had his share, would understand. He died at the wonderful age of 88 in 1984.

John Laurie

When I first met John Laurie, who played the local undertaker in Walmington, and in uniform Private Fraser, I was slightly intimidated by him – John Laurie, I mean, not Private Fraser. He breezed into the rehearsal room on that first morning and was briefly introduced to those he didn't already know, myself among them, and in a short sharp response said, 'Hello son, pleased to meet you,' and was away to corner of the room where he had left his hat and coat and newspaper. That newspaper was almost his trademark. A copy of *The Times* was his comforter and woe betide anybody who went near it. He immediately went to work on the crossword. As the *Dad's Army* years went on it became a race between John, Joan Lowe and Ian Lavender as to who would finish the crossword first. I think that it was the crossword more than anything that really intimidated me. I don't think I had ever tried to read *The Times*, let alone dare to look at the crossword! I wondered what sort of conversation I could ever hope to have with someone who did *The Times* crossword. There was no wasting of time with John – if the rehearsal wasn't going to start there and then, it was crossword time. First impressions can be deceptive and so it turned out to be with John Laurie. Once you got to know him he was, of course, just another actor, slightly eccentric perhaps, but intelligent and outspoken, which you accepted.

Very early into the first rehearsals, John said to Jimmy Perry, the co-writer, 'I hope this is going to work, laddie. To my mind it's a ridiculous idea, a programme about the Home Guard.' Well, there's candour for you – and

John Laurie with his pet chickens. *(Peter Way)*

after having accepted the part he was playing, too! Within a few short weeks it became obvious that *Dad's Army* was taking off and John had to retract his words. Without fear of shame or embarrassment, he said to Jimmy, 'I never had any doubts that it wouldn't succeed.' He dismissed his first remark by making this very obvious contradiction of it. In other words, he turned it into a sort of joke, as did the writers. That little true-life incident became a comedy situation for the whole series. When Captain Mainwaring was proposing some exercise or another which seemed far-fetched to most and quite stupid to Private Fraser, he would say 'It's folly, sheer folly, it'll never work, the man's mad.' When it did eventually work out in some extraordinary way, and most of the other members of the platoon were saying, 'I don't know how you managed it Captain Mainwaring,' or some such flattering remark, Fraser would jump straight in with 'I never had any doubts at all

'We're doomed I tell you doomed'

that Mainwaring wouldn't pull it off.'

John Laurie came to *Dad's Army* after a long and distinguished career in theatre and films. He was born in Dumfries and was destined for a career in architecture, but then came World War I. He talked very little about this episode in his life, but from the little he did say about that war he thought that men should not have been put through such terrible experiences. He said he never expected to come out of it alive. After being invalided out of the services, he finished his war as a sergeant-of-arms at the Tower of London. Architecture, or the thought of it, seemed a thing of the past by 1919 and John decided to become an actor in the theatre. He did his initial studies at Stratford-on-Avon where he

'Could it be an intruder after my gold pieces? John Laurie as Fraser in 'The Miser's Hoard' *(BBC)*

pursued his love of Shakespeare and he was determined to become an actor. His Scottish single-mindedness paid off, for although he didn't play any Scottish parts for many years, as he had intended eventually he played all the great Shakespearean roles at the Old Vic and at Stratford. His King Lear was thought to be one of the great performances on the British stage. He went into films in 1930 when he worked for Alfred Hitchcock in that director's first talkie *Juno and the Paycock*. He worked with Hitchcock again on the memorable and original *Thirty-nine Steps*, starring that wonderful actor Robert Donat, whose life was shortened by continual asthma attacks. Other versions of the *Thirty-nine Steps* have been filmed since then and Robert Powell has starred as the central character Hannay in a television version.

John said that Alfred Hitchcock was an extraordinary man and although he (John) never crossed swords with him, he could be very frightening to work with.

The film industry here and in the USA was expanding rapidly and John was part of it when he played the Mad Mahdi in Zolton Korda's early classic *The Four Feathers* (the Mad Mahdi cropped up again later in *Dad's Army*). John also featured in Alexander Korda's (Zoltan's brother) *Bonnie Prince Charlie*. When the various television companies are showing some of the old classic film comedies, you will see John in one or two of them with, for instance, Will Hay, playing slightly eccentric characters. John was forever grateful that he had had the chance to work with Laurence Olivier, whom he admired tremendously, and the wonderful experience of

'Whatever next?': the Warden and Fraser disguised as tribesmen in 'Two and a Half Feathers'.
(Lynn News)

appearing in his Shakespearean films, *Richard III*, *Hamlet* and *Henry V*. He used to say that when he watched the film of *Henry V* the battle scenes made his hair stand on end. He thought it was a masterpiece of photography and atmosphere.

It took quite a long time for me to find out anything about John. It was not that he couldn't be bothered to talk about all the marvellous things he had done, he just thought it was all in the past and people didn't want to listen to, as he would say, 'the ramblings of an old man'. Occasionally, I did find a way to draw him out. I would tell him how much I admired all the great classical actors and that I certainly hadn't got the talent or even the inclination to tangle with that side of the 'game'. John would then be happy to tell me all about the actors he had worked with

and in doing so he naturally talked about his involvement with them and the productions he had been in. However it took me the best part of nine years to find this all out.

On the way to the studio from Buckingham to do a recording, John had had an accident in his car. He was obviously shaken and had several cuts about the face, but, being the proud Scotsman that he was, after being patched up he insisted on coming in to do the recording. He took the day fairly easily, but it still takes something out of your nervous system to do any performance, and to do it after you've been in a car crash and when you are no youngster (he was already then into his seventies) takes some courage.

On another occasion when we were filming an episode, John and I were playing a couple of desert Bedouins in a flash-back sequence that involved Corporal Jones' experiences with General Gordon and the Mad Mahdi in Khartoum. This sequence was being filmed near King's Lynn in Norfolk in some huge sandpits to simulate the desert. John and I were on horseback and had to ride at a leisurely pace into an open space beyond some high dunes. Film sequences were being prepared on the other side of the dunes, so John and I took the opportunity to get used to the horses. I was, and still am, very raw in the saddle (no pun) but John was an experienced horseman. However, even the most docile of animals can sometimes be disturbed and this is exactly what happened. Suddenly, a couple of practice rifle shots rang out from the other side of the dune and John's horse bolted. He managed after a time to bring it under control and pacify the animal, but I know he was shaken by the mishap. I asked him if he

The lugubrious undertaker from Walmington-on-Sea, Private Fraser (alias John Laurie). Private Fraser was the cynical observer of Captain Mainwaring's foibles and had a pessimistic outlook on life – 'We're doomed, I tell you, doomed!' *(David Croft)*

would like to go back to the caravans for a rest and a cup of tea, but he said, 'No, laddie, I'll be all right, and don't mention it to the others, I don't want any fuss.' And that just about summed John up. I think he believed he might break down and not be able to carry on at all if anyone started showing concern or sympathising with him, which of course would have been the case because we were a caring company.

After rehearsals, John would dash off back to his home in Buckinghamshire which was his anchorage. He lived very quietly there with his wife Oonah, and, when she was home, his attractive daughter Veronica. He kept horses himself and the lovely setting of that country house where he could relax in the autumn of his life and walk with his dogs had, as he said, been earned from a lifetime of acting. There is a story about John which I never heard him deny, possibly because he used to like to hear people chuckling about it, which I'm sure he quite enjoyed. On Saturday mornings he would put a notice outside his house saying 'Manure for sale – 2s 6d a bag', and he would personally serve the customers himself because he said it boosted sales. Was this a ploy copied from the American comedian Jack Benny, whose supposed thrift served him well as far as publicity was concerned for many years, or was it just good business sense inherent in all Scots? Whichever way, it caused great amusement to those who knew about it. By 1968 and prior to his call up in *Dad's Army*, John would almost certainly have settled for semi-retirement, just doing the occasional radio play or a poetry-reading which he enjoyed. He always said that this new career in television was a bonus at his time of life.

He was not stretched too far, and most of the time rehearsals were fairly leisurely, apart from the filming sessions in Norfolk and recording days in the studio.

One of the delights for us, and I know the viewing public, were his dramatic stories about a supposed experience which he would launch into if the platoon were in a tight spot on some night patrol. This would bring terror to Corporal Jones and Private Pike. With his eyes flashing he would say, 'We're doomed, I tell you. I remember the time on the lonely Isle of Barra, the wind whistling round the headland and there in the silence of the mist it appeared. Bloodshot eyes, a huge body and a long tail, creeping nearer and nearer.' And then just as everyone was in a state of paralysed fear, he would scream out 'We're doomed, I tell you, doomed, doomed.' Of

course, there would always be a perfectly simple explanation for the monster or whatever phantom he had suggested.

I shall always remember John Laurie as a larger-than-life character with a natural personality for making even ordinary dialogue sound extraordinary. I wish I had had the opportunity of seeing him in some of the great Shakespearean roles – it must have been an education.

Top right: **John Laurie filming in Norfolk.**

Below: **John Laurie relaxing at his Buckinghamshire home** *(Peter Way)*

James Beck

An early theatrical idol of mine was the great comedian Sid Field. Jimmy Beck was also a fan of Sid's and I remember his surprise one day when I said to him that if the Sid Field story was ever produced, he would be a natural for the part. At times Jim looked very much like Sid, but it wasn't just the obvious parallel of one of Sid's funniest characters, the spiv 'Slasher Green' and Jimmy's Private Walker in *Dad's Army* – they both, in fact, had that mischievous look of 'What can I get up to next?' about them. Jimmy had done his preliminary training in the provinces just as Sid had before coming to London and finding fame, Sid with his very successful revues at The Prince of Wales Theatre and Jimmy through the medium of television. The similarity of coincidence did not stop there; for they both died in their early forties before they had a chance to really capitalise on their potential. Sid would have been a natural for situation comedy in post-war television. Jimmy did have success in that area, but would almost certainly have gone on to other more serious aspects of the theatre, as was promised by his earlier critical acclaim in repertory.

Jimmy was born in London in 1929 in the middle of the Depression. His father was a tram-driver and became one of the millions of unemployed at that time. This left Jimmy's mother to become the breadwinner, which she did by making artificial flowers which were fashionable at that time. His great dislike of artificial flora stemmed from his early childhood, probably because he associated them with his mother's struggle to make ends meet. Jimmy's wife, Kay, told me that if he couldn't

have fresh flowers in their house he wouldn't have any. He went to art school when he was fourteen and enjoyed that part of his life, which is not surprising because he became a very good painter and sculptor. Examples of his work adorn the lovely cottage he and Kay shared for many years, and where Kay still lives.

Jimmy left home at seventeen and soon decided he wanted to go into the theatre. He had been interested in it since he was a youngster and had compiled a scrap-book of film and stage stars which is still intact. It is crammed full of pictures and press cuttings and chit-chat of the greats in cinema and theatre. He was called up, as all young men were in their late teens, and he did his national service as a PT instructor. When his service was completed, he started on the serious business of looking for work in the theatre. He obtained engagements with several repertory companies and it was his contracts with the York Theatre Company that was a turning point for him. He became a leading man for that company playing in *A View from the Bridge* and Shylock in *The Merchant of Venice*, Archie Rice in *The Entertainer* (for which he received a congratulatory letter from the originator Laurence Olivier) and other major roles.

It was while Jimmy was at York that he met his wife-to-be. The company did short seasons at Scarborough on the North Yorkshire coast and Kay was living in the resort after she had separated from her first husband. After their initial meeting, Jimmy would often cycle from York to Scarborough to meet her, which was no mean feat on a bicycle. Jimmy felt he had done all he could at York so decided to come back to London as soon as he and Kay

Walker: '**I've got some very good knicker elastic. How about some for your wife, Captain Mainwaring?**'

Mainwaring: '**How dare you, Walker!**'

Walker: '**Well, you can't get it in the shops, you know.**'

were married. Further repertory seasons followed, but Jimmy still felt that he wasn't being stretched. It is perhaps essential that an actor should always feel he could do more and do it better than his or her contemporaries, particularly someone like Jimmy whose whole life was now the theatre and who became bored if he was not working. He loved watching a great performance and admired talented actors. He was well versed in opera and could quote whole passages in whichever language the particular opera was in. On holidays abroad he could pick up the language quite easily – that in itself is a gift. I do wonder whether the actor's sense of frustration, which is an understandable part of their creative talent, can sometimes be a drawback and

unsettle them. I believe it did this to Jimmy more than occasionally. He did not seem to be totally satisfied with his part in *Dad's Army*, even though he was very successful in it. The general public really loved the character of Private Walker the Spiv. They remembered with great affection that sort of cheeky con-man type from the war years. The spiv had an element of excitement about him and he was very useful in the black market economy, gently flouting the law. Jimmy had the built-in excitement in his make up to make the character very believable. He was still going back into the theatre on occasions in the early days of the series and I know that John Le Mesurier and Clive Dunn went to the Palace Theatre, Watford, to see him acting in *Staircase*, and

James Beck and John Le Mesurier during filming for 'Two and a Half Feathers' *(Eastern Evening News)*

James Beck as the incorrigible Private Walker. His performances as the slick spiv, wheeling and dealing in black market goods, caught the public imagination. *(David Croft)*

they both said he was brilliant.

By 1972 Jimmy had had several offers as a result of his exposure in the series and they started to come to fruition in 1973. He had his own series with London Weekend Television called *Romany Jones*, he did a couple of one-off comedy hours with Ronnie Fraser, he was asked to make an LP record of Cockney songs and he was featured reading stories for BBC TV's *Jackanory*. At this time the BBC had made the important decision to rerecord some of the old Tony Hancock scripts. Arthur Lowe was to play the Hancock character (in his own style, of course) and Jimmy Beck would play the Sid James role. Ray Galton and Alan Simpson, the original writers for Tony Hancock both on radio and television, were already updating the Hancock scripts to accommodate the two actors' styles. I knew Arthur and Jimmy were both excited about the project, but alas, it never came about, nor did a further series of *Romany Jones* or any of the other projects destined for Jimmy. He died in 1973. He was taken ill the day after we had been recording some BBC radio episodes of *Dad's Army* at the Playhouse Theatre in Northumberland Avenue. That Friday night was the last time any of us saw him.

There are several things I personally remember about Jimmy. He would come into the rehearsal rooms in the mornings, stand almost still, summing up the atmosphere, then flash his toothy smile and more often than not start the day with an impression of Humphrey Bogart, Edward G. Robinson or W.C. Fields. It was his way of saying, 'I'm in a good mood, I hope you are.' One night when we were away filming, John Le Mesurier met an old friend from his Army days – a colonel or similar high-ranking officer – in the bar of the hotel and invited him up to his room for a nightcap, and Jimmy joined them. I didn't know that John had company, but that night I decided to play a joke on him (my room was directly opposite his) and I walked across to his room stark naked except for my boots and white helmet. Realising that I had made a gaffe and that the Army officer was fairly shocked, I retreated very quickly, but Jimmy Beck who had been standing by the door got to my room first, slammed it shut and locked me out in the corridor. We all became rather hysterical, including the officer, mostly out of sheer embarrassment. The one worry now was that Arthur Lowe, whose room was just down the corridor, would come out and see what was going on at 1 o'clock in the morning, so I hid in a broom cupboard for several minutes until John and Jimmy had telephoned reception to get a pass key from the night porter. When he came up Jimmy said to him, 'The warden has just been visiting the vicar' (who was played, of course by, Frank Williams). I hoped the night porter wasn't a religious man.

Jimmy's wife Kay told me that one day when they were in York she and Jimmy were going into 'Betty's', a favourite and rather sophisticated tea-room in the city, and as they were going in Jimmy started talking to a tramp (they always interested him) and invited him in for tea. 'Betty's' were not over-happy about this but accommodated Jimmy's new-found 'friend'. The family cat was certainly a friend and on one occasion when he rang Kay at home to find out how the cat was, I asked him 'And how's Kay?'. He said, 'Fine, I think,' and after a moment's hesitation added, 'Hold on, I'll go and ring up the cat and make sure.'

Kay was a truly supportive theatrical wife, the type of person who stayed behind the scenes but was always available to help Jimmy make decisions and give him confidence, which he did not have in abundance, even though he knew what he wanted. It is very easy when you're caught up in the day-to-day business of television or theatre literally to forget to eat or even have a regular meal pattern. Kay is a smashing cook, her toasted muffins are delicious, and she always made sure that Jimmy ate well and had a secure life when he was at home.

James Beck with his wife Kay and the family cat. *(Kay Beck)*

Ian Lavender

Ian Lavender who was cast as Private Pike, the youngest member of the platoon. Private Pike not only had to suffer the fussing of his mother, who always made him where a scarf on patrol, but also tended to jeopardize Captain Mainwaring's plans; hence the rejoinder 'You stupid boy!'.

Many people imagined that it was Warden Hodges who was mostly on the receiving end of the *Dad's Army* custard pies, but if you were to sit through a selection of a dozen random episodes you would realise that it was 'Pikey' who took the greater proportion of them. Mainwaring, having got him into most of those ludicrous situations, would then add insult to injury with that most unforgettable of pay-off lines 'You stupid boy'.

Ian Lavender, however, is anything but a stupid boy. He is a dab-hand at crosswords, a very good back-gammon player and a real Do-It-Yourself fiend. I used to drop into his house for a cup of tea on occasions and was amazed at his handiwork. Ian put in his own central heating system and rewired the house from top to bottom. Self-taught from manuals, he makes the doing of it sound all so easy.

Ian was born in Birmingham exactly nine months after V-Day in 1945. It seems that his parents did rather more celebrating on that day than most! Ian's father was a policeman in Birmingham during World War II, mainly dealing with unexploded bombs and other weird devices that had been dropped from the sky. Cadbury's Bourneville Trust came into Ian's life at quite an early age. The Quaker family not only originated the famous Bourneville village with tree-lined roads and other amenities for Birmingham, but they also financed four technical schools that taught almost any subject. All the sports grounds were supported by Cadbury's with excellent facilities that no other schools in Birmingham had at that time.

At the age of seven, Ian wanted to be an actor. At junior school he got the plum part of Mozart in a play because he was taking piano lessons, even though he could only play twenty-eight bars of music. He also played Pontious Pilot in an Easter pageant, based on *A Man Born to be King*, because his mother and father had a copy of a radio script, so it was a case of 'It's my bat and my ball so I should have the best part' – and why not? It was all part of a childhood ambition to tread the boards.

Ian went straight from senior school to the Bristol Old Vic Drama School, a venue particularly revered by so many actors and actresses who have passed through it. Ian had obtained a grant from the City of Birmingham, a corporation that has always been generous in this direction if they believed a drama student would make good use of it. As he said, 'That was the luck of living in Birmingham.'

Ian thoroughly enjoyed his time at Bristol and when he finished there his talent and potential was quickly recognised. Almost immediately he had the offer of three jobs. Canterbury seemed to be the most attractive, so he started a six-month engagement at the old Marlow Theatre in that beautiful city. After Canterbury he made his first television appearance. Ian was sent the script only the day before the first rehearsals began, so assuming that it was a very small part, cast at the last minute, he didn't even bother to look at it until he arrived at rehearsals. To his astonishment, therefore, he discovered that he was playing the lead. There was no 'It's my bat and my ball' in that situation. The television play was called *Flowers at my Feet* and Ian enjoyed it, working with a lovely cast who were most helpful to him.

Very shortly after this he was cast as Private Pike in *Dad's Army* and the first filming sequence was to be shot at Thetford. Ian arrived at BBC Television Centre to pick up the coach with all the other actors and, being inexperienced, thought they would all return that same day. When he realised that everyone had suitcases, he had to dash back home and pack a few things, because this was the first of the many location stays at the Bell Hotel in Thetford.

In the filming for the first episode all the dialogue was to be mute, but when it was realised that some of the action that was going to be reserved for the studio could be done there, Ian had to say a few lines, which he naturally hadn't learnt, together with the rest of the 'gang', so he had to quickly study his part and find a suitable voice. The one he tried out first time seemed to please everyone, so the plaintive 'Mr Mainwaring ... etc', was heard for the first time, and he stuck with it for the next nine years. Those nine years he does not regret for it was a period in his life when he came to theatrical maturity.

The first few months of *Dad's Army* were exciting for everyone, but in particular for Ian, a young man on the threshold of a television career and in the company of some fine actors in a top television series. As Ian said, 'It was a team show. Even though all the individual actors were

Mainwaring: 'Don't stand there gaping boy, it's probably one of ours'
L to R: Ian Lavender,, Arthur Lowe
(Independent Free Press)

Mainwaring: 'Now listen Pike, it's my turn to man the bren gun today, and I'll be covering the High Street from Timothy Whites to the Novelty Rock Emporium'. Arthur Lowe/Mainwaring; Ian Lavender/Pike; John Le Mesurier/ Wilson *(BBC)*

so different in their outlook, they all got on well with each other. There was a rapport between some more than others.' John Laurie and Ian were great chums, discussing the business of acting, doing the crossword together and sometimes travelling together to locations. Ian was inclined to look after John, in the nicest possible way, and John looked on Ian as a son who was always ready to absorb the experience of John's knowledge. The character of Pikey was never going to be easy to play, particularly for an inexperienced actor. In the bank he was a very junior clerk under Manager Mainwaring and this junior position was carried on into the Home Guard, but at the same time 'Pikey' had to

emerge as a personality as far as the viewing public was concerned. Ian would be the first to agree that he had some great lines and situations given to him which allowed him to emerge so strongly in the part.

It was inevitable that Ian would be typecast for a while after the series finished, but he has certainly proved through a variety of roles since that he is not 'a stupid boy' and in 1989 he appeared in London alongside Dustin Hoffman in *The Merchant of Venice.*

Ian has two sons, Daniel and Sam, and they are a great credit to him and their mother Suzanne. I know John Laurie was very proud to be Daniel's godfather and, incidentally, so am I.

The Antagonists

Frank Williams

Frank Williams has always been tall, certainly six foot plus, so his first professional engagement must have been very uncomfortable for he played two parts at the Gateway Theatre in London: a snail and an ant.

Born in North London where he has lived all his life, Frank had a happy childhood and his own disposition was probably responsible for this. He is fun to be with and people laugh with him even when, as Clive Dunn would comment, 'he gets in a bit of a muddle'. At the age of twelve Frank went to Ardingly College in Sussex as a boarder. He avoided all sports because he found ball games frightening; (even now his comment on people who play cricket is to the point, rather like a Greyfriars pupil of the 'Bunter' ilk, 'look out chaps, they've got one of those nasty hard things they're throwing about', followed by 'come away Teddy, you'll get hurt' – some of us used to have a little practice in the lunch breaks). At Ardingly he dodged sports by joining the school Land Army, digging potatoes etc, even on very cold days. He was interested in drama, but it was not taught at Ardingly. The Junior Training Corps was compulsory for pupils, but Frank was not keen on its activities; on mock manoeuvres he said: 'You were able to get out of marching and all that stuff by getting captured early on and having a lie down in the sun until all the silly business was finished.'

Frank is very intelligent and regrets that he did not go to university. He became an inveterate cinema-goer and theatre buff and as soon as he had left school, with very good academic qualifications, he decided to enter the theatre. Not only did he perform in other writers' plays at the Gateway Theatre, but in 1952 he wrote his first play which was produced there with some success. In 1955 he was cast in a television play by R.F. Delderfield (the author of *Worm's Eye View*). At about this time he also appeared in his first film. In 1957 he worked at the Palace Theatre, Watford, which was run by Jimmy and Gilda Perry. This was the start of a long association with them both. Two of his plays were produced at Watford under the Perry management.

Cast in one episode of the highly successful *Army Game* for television, Frank was brought back very quickly into the series as an army officer, Captain Pocket. He played that role for seventy episodes in that very funny series. *The Army Game* brought Frank a certain amount of fame and security. He has performed a variety of roles in the theatre from the classics to panto-mime dame, and played many parts in both film and television productions in his own particular style. When he first joined the cast of *Dad's Army*, he immediately stamped his authority on the character of the vicar of Walmington-on-Sea.

Frank has worked mainly in the theatre in recent years, including three seasons with the English Stage Company in Vienna. Two of his own plays, *Murder by Appointment* in 1985 and a long national tour of *Alibi for Murder* in 1989,

'One volunteer who lacked a steel helmet, to satisfy a nervous wife left home in the Blitz to come on duty wearing a piece of enamel-wear on his head, secured by a scarf'.

North West (London) Frontier. A History of No. 6 Company, 23rd Middlesex Battalion, Home Guard.

Frank Williams as the Vicar of Walmington-on-Sea. The Vicar and his accomplice, the Verger, often clashed with Captain Mainwaring over the use of the church hall. *(David Croft)*

have had successful runs.

Frank is also a lay preacher and works very hard for his local church, so it is surprising to discover that he is a gregarious character and something of an adventurer. Frank likes nothing better than to have a social evening with friends in a restaurant in the presence of amusing com-

pany, and he will make up for any jollity that is lacking in that company. He stores up stories of funny situations and laughs uncontrollably when he recalls them – for instance, there is a story that begins 'Do you remember when John Le Mesurier, Teddy Sinclair, Bill Pertwee and I booked into a hotel in Birmingham when we were on tour with the stage show of *Dad's* and it became obvious that the hotel was used quite a lot by ladies of easy virtue and we had to tell Teddy we were going to move out? It hadn't dawned on the innocent Ted as to why, even though he did say he couldn't sleep for doors being opened and shut all night!.'

When Frank is on tour he often stays with the local vicar and his family, many of whom he has become acquainted with through the Actors Church Union, a branch of the clergy that pays regular visits to theatres back-stage. This custom goes back a long way to the time when, in the days of low wages, the local vicar would help to sort out accommodation and other problems for the visiting actors. As a committee member of Equity, the actors' union, Frank has also done a great deal of work on behalf of his fellow artistes.

The partnership of the vicar and the verger, always slightly subordinate to 'His Reverence', was an inspired piece of casting. The fact that the vicar had loaned the church hall to Mainwaring on certain evenings would always cause some aggravation because there would be occasions when both would want the hall for their own activities – Mainwaring's platoon with weapon training, etc, and the vicar with organising a choir practice. One of my favourite episodes was 'The Godiva Affair'. The vicar was chairman of the committee that had to select a girl to play Lady Godiva in a pageant that was being presented to raise money for one of the wartime funds. Captain Mainwaring came out of his office at the sound of giggling and in the hall was confronted by several young ladies in bathing costumes. The air raid warden was present and Mainwaring discovered him leering at the ladies. Mainwaring admonished the warden as follows: 'How dare you have naked girls in here, cover them up.' The vicar seemed not to be concerned by the situation and replied: 'Don't be absurd, all this fuss over a few silly girls.' The verger replied as follows: 'Yes, if the vicar wants to have silly girls in his hall that's his affair.' Very often the vicar used the verger to spy on Mainwaring's camp. He would pretend to be dusting or doing some other ineffectual duty, but at the same time he would be peering around corners trying to pick up odd bits of information to pass on to the vicar, or if he felt particularly ill-disposed towards Mainwaring at the time, he would also inform Hodges, the warden, who would use that information to Mainwaring's disadvantage. So very often the vicar, verger and warden would all gang up against the platoon. The warden was always receptive to any idea that would give him a chance to get the better of 'Napoleon', his favourite term of reference for Mainwaring.

Warden Hodges believed that he should be in charge of Walmington-on-Sea in an emergency, but he never had the respect of the townspeople to do this, even if he had had the courage, which he lacked. Hodges, the target of Mainwaring's derisory remarks such as 'What can you expect, he's a greengrocer with dirty finger nails', was basically a coward, as opposed to Mainwaring who epitomised the bulldog breed living in Britain in the 1940s.

Nothing seemed impossible, and although it was more optimism than anything else, Mainwaring was convinced that he could hold Walmington against a German invasion with his conviction that 'He who holds Walmington-on-Sea holds this island.'

The Vicar and the Verger, *Dad's Army's* **Stan and Ollie.** *(Radio Times)*

Edward Sinclair

Known as the quiet man of *Dad's Army*, Ted Sinclair was unique. His character of the verger was a finely drawn piece of observation. Edward, or Teddy as he was known to us, only had to enter a scene in his flowing cassock with its wide belt and familiar yellow duster hanging from it, with a flat cap on his head, and the audience was immediately in the mood to laugh. Ted had a particular song in his voice that gave the verger's character an added dimension. He was meticulous, almost fussy, as an actor and that was his strength. His experience had come from years in the theatre. Ted's parents were touring repertory players from 1914 until the late 1920s and he was taken on stage when they were performing when he was only six months old. Ted's mother was also a pianist and singer, which obviously had a bearing on his talent for writing lyrics.

Ted realised at a very early age that acting was a precarious business, so he did the next best thing and joined an amateur company in the 1930s and played and directed for them with great success in plays as diverse as *The Admirable Crichton, Rookery Nook, The Rivals, Busman's Honeymoon* and *Twelfth Night*.

He was tempted to join the professional ranks but declined the offers he was made. He was called up into the Army in 1940 and soon found himself in service concert parties playing to the troops. Demobbed in 1945, he took up where he had left off in amateur dramatics. By the 1950s Ted was married with young children and was still resisting the temptation to turn professional as he wanted to secure a future for his family. He had a very good job as a top salesman and was happy to bide his time.

When his sons Peter and Keith were firmly settled into a good education, with his wife Gladys providing a stable home life, Ted finally took the plunge and became a professional.

He appeared as Barkiss in the television serial of *David Copperfield* and then featured in various comedy programmes, including those of David Croft. Following this, David cast him as the verger in *Dad's Army*.

Ted and Frank Williams became a great team in the production and their friendship spread to their off-stage activities. They would drive to film locations together in Ted's

Edward Sinclair whose characterisation of the Verger was finely observed. He only had to enter a scene dressed in his cassock to make an audience laugh.
(David Croft)

car and he would accommodate Frank's collection of books, a very heavy and almost antique video recorder, and suitcases full of clothes, etc, which would leave Ted with little room for his own belongings. One day I passed them driving up the A1 to Baldock en route to a filming sometimes make up Ted's mind for him when he was being hesitant in making a decision. It was the perfect working combination and all was done with great good humour. Ted and his wife Gladys were certainly the perfect married couple and I know that his two sons were

The author/Air Raid Warden Hodges trying to learn his lines for the next scene. Fred McNaughton/the Mayor looks on: 'The Royal Train' *(Brian Fisher)*

session; they were doing about twenty-five miles an hour and Frank was trying to read a huge map which seemed to envelope them both, while at the same time he was talking non-stop to Teddy. Ted would get involved with Frank's mishaps, and Frank would then complain to everyone: 'If only Teddy had listened to me, we would have been alright.' On the other hand, Frank would very proud of their father. His death just after we finished the final episode of the series in 1977 was a tremendous shock to us all, although I knew that he had struggled with indifferent health for many years. Ted never made a fuss about his illness and at times it took a great deal of courage for him to carry on a normal acting career which physically is always very demanding.

The Back Row of the Chorus

It was obvious from the outset that there would have to be regular platoon personnel in the Walmington-on-Sea Home Guard. After all, it would be strange if new faces kept cropping up, which certainly would not have happened in reality as most males had been called up for service in the armed forces during the war, leaving behind the fairly old and the young. The same had to apply to the television platoon and it became essential to find male actors who would be available for several series – if the programme ran that long – actors who for most of the time would have little or no dialogue but who would regularly be involved in the action. It was necessary that these actors should be able to take the odd line when it was needed, so they had to be actors of experience. The final selection was very interesting.

Hugh Hastings, one of the stalwarts of the platoon. *(Alan Howard Photography)*

Hugh Hastings, had earned high plaudits in the theatre as a playwright with his very successful West End production of *Seagulls over Sorrento*, a naval play which starred John Gregson, Ronnie Shiner (star of the long running *Worm's Eye View*), Bernard Lee (M in the James Bond films), William Hartnell (the first Dr Who) and Nigel Stock (Dr Watson in various Sherlock Holmes stories). *Seagulls over Sorrento* ran for hundreds of performances in London and had some success in America where it starred Rod Steiger. The play was eventually adapted by Hugh into a musical, *Scapa*, which opened at the Adelphi Theatre in London and starred Pete Murray and Edward Woodward.

Hugh came to England from Australia in 1936 and followed his parents' musical tradition by playing the piano in a band at Blackpool before he went into repertory at Dundee where Charlotte Frances taught him most of what he knows about the theatre. Hugh joined the Navy at the outbreak of World War II and had the worst day of his life on the abortive Dieppe raid which had been planned as a mini rehearsal for the second front at a later date. After the war Hugh went into revue with Hermione Gingold and then enjoyed an astonishing success with *Seagulls over Sorrento*. The euphoria of this production, even though it lasted for some time, did not sustain him forever, and he became a cabaret artiste in night-clubs where he played the piano and sang his own songs (Hugh had been writing lyrics since the age of fifteen when he was working on a sheep farm in Australia.) He then accompanied Sarah Churchill on cabaret dates and later became my accompanist in concerts in the Seventies after I had met him in *Dad's Army*. During the run of the series he had had the good fortune to appear in John Osborne's *Sense of Detachment* which brought him to the notice of Frank Dunlop's Young Vic Company with whom he toured all over the world. Hugh has a one-man show which he has taken on a UK tour.

Colin Bean (who played Private Sponge) began as one of the back row of the chorus but gradually assumed a more prominent role in various episodes. Jimmy Perry arrived at the name for this character when he saw the word 'Sponge' over a shop and thought it was unusual and attractive.

Colin Bean was trained at the Northern Theatre School, Bradford, where some of his classmates included Robert Stephens, Tom Bell and Bernard Hepton. He made his initial radio appearances in Japan, where he was stationed with the British forces. Colin returned home to seasons of repertory at Sheffield in the company of Paul Eddington and Bernard Archard, before he moved on to a long stint with Harry Hanson's Court Players. Colin first met Jimmy Perry at the Palace Theatre, Watford, and later Jimmy remembered the hard-working and affable Colin and invited him to join the television platoon. Colin is now based in Lancashire and works regularly for a Northern theatre company in that area, including presenting his one-man performance of *A Gradley Neet*.

Michael Moore was a well-known radio and theatre actor in the Forties and Fifties, mainly because of his appearances in radio's *Ignorance is Bliss*, which also included Harold Berens and Gladys Hay and introduced the Chairman, Eamonn Andrews, to the listening public.

Leslie Noyes, an ex-variety performer and a good-natured stooge to Arthur Haynes in stage and television productions, was another asset to the platoon, as was **George Hancock**, a retired opera singer who could still sing an aria in his deep bass voice. **Richard Jaques**, actor, director and pianist; **Ewan Evans**, singer with a store of Welsh anecdotes; **Jimmy Mac**, with the irresistible smile and gag a minute that he could recall from his vast experience in music hall and pantomime; **Roger Bourne**, Jimmy Perry's old friend from Collins Music Hall; **Hugh Cecil**, a children's entertainer who had brought

many happy hours to youngsters of all ages, particularly at the seaside; **Vernon Drake**, part of a very famous music hall double act, Connor and Drake, **Frank Godfrey**, formerly manager of the Palace Theatre, Watford, and **Desmond Callum-Jones**, a big man with a big car and who had a little financial independence tucked away in the form of property – all made up this marvellous and friendly group of lads who were determined to help stop 'Hitler's Army' from landing. The amount of entertainment that these professionals could jointly have provided would have enabled them to put on a show in their own right. They did lose **Vic Taylor** who sadly died during the early days of the series, but even in the short time that he was with the platoon, he proved a tremendous asset, particularly with all the filming sequences. A very nice gentleman was Vic.

Sponge: 'Look out! Here comes the Captain!'
L to R: Colin Bean as Private Sponge and Ian Lavender as Private Pike

Welcome Guests

Harold Bennett

Harold quite regularly made guest appearances as the old character Mr Bluett, who was not going to fall in with all the alarmist notions that were put about in Walmington-on-Sea. Mr Bluett would show great impatience at being aroused in the middle of the night just to please Mainwaring's mob in search of a lost gun or at the warden's excitable warnings and banging on the doors because he believed that German bombers were approaching. Harold appeared in reality to be a frail old gentleman, but when it came to playing his part, he was dominating and forthright without any sign of hesitancy. Harold went on to play the Young Mr Grace (in his eighties) for the entire run of the comedy series *Are You Being Served?* He was supposed to be in his eighties then, so goodness knows what age the 'Old Mr Grace' was supposed to be. Although Harold Bennett was a senior citizen himself, he played regularly in the London theatres.

Felix Bowness

Many thousands of people who have been part of a television studio audience over the years will probably have experienced the disjointed volley of quips, jokes, racing tips and general audience participation from Felix Bowness as he warmed up an audience. The first appearance he had in a small role in *Dad's Army* was just as frenetic and caused us to wonder whether he was wound up in the morning with a key and let loose on the world like a clockwork toy.

Felix has been an entertainer for nearly forty years in variety and summer shows all around the country (very often in his favourite resort, the Isle of Wight), playing in pantomime and cabaret and giving after-dinner speeches. It was Benny Hill who suggested that Felix would make a good warm-up man, or studio host as they are now called, and he has warmed up something like five thousand television productions. In one week Felix has worked for as many as fifteen different studio shows. On one particularly fraught evening, he began by warming up the audience for *Wogan* at the BBC Theatre in Shepherd's Bush at 7pm and then jumping on a motorbike to dash down to the Thames Television studios at Teddington in Middlesex to warm up the audience for the Des O'Connor show at 8pm. Although studio hosting can be a difficult job at times, Felix's professional approach has earned him the admiration of many top professional actors and the eventual reward of appearances in their shows. After making dozens of small guest appearances in various productions, a regular character was eventually found for him as the jockey Fred Quilley in Jimmy and David's successful *Hi-De-Hi* series. I am sure the part he played in some of the *Dad's Army* episodes helped him in that direction. Initially when he came to the filming sessions in Norfolk, he laughed at the scenes being rehearsed while he was waiting to take his own part, not realising that this was against the rules, for laughter was the studio audience's job. Felix was told to go away and be quiet, so he climbed up a tree and sat in the branches and started to imitate a bird call. Nobody knew that he had done this at the time and when the episode was shown, people believed that there had been a song-bird somewhere within earshot of the microphones.

Felix Bowness who was a guest star in *Dad's Army* **before becoming a regular character in** *Hi-De-Hi.*

In 1986 Felix was warming up the audience for the *This is Your Life* series. It is not an easy job because the audience must be kept amused for a long time while the guest celebrity is brought to the studio from wherever he or she has been surprised, and then sent to the make-up department and even change their clothes. On one such occasion, while Felix was amusing the audience while they were waiting for the guest to arrive, the late Eamonn Andrews came on stage, tapped Felix on the shoulder and said 'Felix Bowness, this is your life'. It was a memorable night for him as his show-business and racing friends came in to offer congratulations.

Felix's career began when he won a talent contest at the old Palace Theatre, Reading. Shortly afterwards Vera Lynn heard him singing and was impressed by his voice. Although she offered to coach him personally at her London home, Felix was determined to make a career as a comedian,

so the 'Atomic Comic', as he called himself, was launched, without a song. In his teens he was ABA (Amateur Boxing Association) Champion for London and Southern Counties for three years running. He still has a great interest in sport, but nowadays mainly in racing horses and he part owns a racehorse with his friend Stan Mellor.

Felix has a son who is a detective with the Hampshire Constabulary, three grandchildren and he still lives in the Reading area with his wife Mavis. When agent Richard Stone took Felix on his books thirty years ago, he said 'I'll make you a star one day.' Although Felix never became a big star, he has won many friends in show business and the racing world. He certainly had more than a few in *Dad's Army*. Long may he continue to warm us all up with his humour.

John Clegg

John Clegg became a regular member of the cast of *It aint*

Janet Davies (with Ian Lavender and John Le Mesurier) who was cast as Mavis Pike, the fussy mother of Frank Pike. However, it was her relationship with Sergeant Wilson which kept audiences guessing.
(BBC)

John Clegg

'alf 'ot Mum! after he featured in a *Dad's Army* episode entitled 'The Great Big Wheel'. This episode was based on some true facts. During the war an inventor suggested the idea that huge wheels, similar to those at fairgrounds, could have rockets fixed to them and in the eventuality of a German invasion force landing in this country, the wheels, which would be radio-controlled, would be manoeuvred into position and then directed across the beaches firing their rockets at the enemy landing forces. Members of the wartime Cabinet and high ranking military personnel attended the demonstration, but it went slightly wrong. The huge wheels could not be controlled properly and went into reverse, scattering the onlookers. The events of this story became the basis of the Dad's Army episode in which John Clegg played the absent-minded radio operator.

Apart from appearing in all fifty-six episodes of *It aint 'alf 'ot Mum!* as la-di-dah Gunner Graham, John has guested in many other television programmes and is also equally at home in the theatre. I have played with him on more than one occasion on stage and he has great command as an actor. The one-man show based on the life and works of Rudyard Kipling is also a credit to his stage-craft.

Pamela Cundell

My first meeting with Pam Cundell was in 1955 when I was in a very small concert party near Yarmouth and Pam was in a smart and sophisticated seaside revue called *Between Ourselves* at nearby Lowestoft. The show was produced by Bill Fraser, who later made a name for himself in films, television and on the West End stage, including the National Theatre. At a later date Pamela became Mrs Fraser.

It was a pleasant surprise to know that she would be playing Mrs Fox in the series, a character who was to become a fairly regular visitor. The sight of Mrs Fox would make Corporal Jones, who ran the butcher's shop in Walmington, become weak at the knees. She played on his romantic emotions for a little favour or two – an extra lamb chop or sausage – over and above her weekly meat ration, In spite of her little wiles, Mrs Fox was a homely and endearing lady which made the character real. Pam Cundell's portrayal of the character was very convincing because she herself is a sincere and warm hearted person.

In one episode, Mrs Fox is invited to the Marigold tea-rooms by Captain Mainwaring who wants to explain to her that Corporal Jones is not concentrating on his Home Guard duties because of his infatuation for her, and that he, Jones, believes that Mrs Fox is flirting with someone else, which she is inclined to do occasionally. However, Mrs Fox thinks Mainwaring has invited her to the tea-rooms to engage in pleasantries himself, perhaps to ask her to take a port and lemon with him one evening and to make some sort of flirtatious advances towards her. The playing of this scene could have been very heavy handed, but with Arthur Lowe's usual deft touch as Mainwaring and the misreading of the situation by Mrs Fox as played by Pam, it became a joy to watch.

Pamela Cundell was trained at the Guildhall School of Music and Drama, after which she has had a varied career in all departments of the entertainment business, making her West End debut in revue at the London Palladium. Film appearances include *Half a*

Sixpence and television programmes with Benny Hill, Frankie Howerd and Harry Worth. Pamela's cry of 'Hello darlings' when she enters a rehearsal studio is always an assurance that everyone will have a jolly time in her company.

Janet Davies

Janet looked like a pretty housewife, someone you would want to come home to, which was exactly what she was intended to be when she was cast as Mavis Pike, mother of Frank Pike, and in a very discreet way the comforter of Sergeant Wilson. Mrs Pike's continual concerns that Frank should not get cold on night duty, that he should have enough to eat and that he should always have his scarf with him were typical of any fussy mother. Mavis would burst into the church hall on parade nights and let fly at Mainwaring with 'My boy is not to be out all night and then get up for work at the bank in the morning. I mean, what about his chest, he's always been delicate since he had the croup', and then quietly say to Sergeant Wilson on her way out, 'And what about you, Arthur, will you be in for your cocoa at the usual time?', which would bring the familiar response from Wilson of 'Please, Mavis', and then he would dismiss her with a gentle wave of his hand.

The way that the situation between Wilson and Mrs Pike was handled appeared to leave little to the imagination, but it was written so well and played so skilfully by Janet that it took some time for the general public to realise the significance of their conversation, but when they did, everyone was part of the secret. The viewers at home liked to think that they had discovered a clandestine relationship, although it was never confirmed. Mainwaring occasionally referred to it when he and Wilson were having a quiet tête-à-tête in the office, but even then there was only a slight suggestion in his questioning and certainly no conclusions were drawn from it.

Born of a Welsh father and Cockney mother, Janet Davies' career began in repertory at Northampton, Watford and Leatherhead, and she was also a popular member of the Theatre Clwdd company. Her London theatre seasons included *The Love Match* with Arthur Askey at the Victoria Palace and *Saturday Night at the Crown* at the Garrick Theatre. Janet was also very proud to have been featured in the film version of *Under Milk Wood* with Richard Burton. Although she had guested in other comedy productions such as *The Last of the Summer Wine* and the *Dick Emery Show*, I am sure she will best be remembered for her appearances as Mrs Pike in *Dad's Army*.

Don Estelle

A very little man walked into the first day's rehearsal for the episode entitled 'Big Guns', but nobody knew him, apart from Arthur Lowe, and then only as a passing acquaintance. This quiet man, who was later to show great entrepreneurial flair, was Don Estelle. Don's climb from a North of England club singer and carpet salesman to television fame is quite extraordinary.

Don was playing one of the extras in 'the crowd' in a costume drama at Granada Television which starred Arthur Lowe and Jim Dale. Wanting to better his lot in show business and being a fan of *Dad's Army*, Don followed Arthur Lowe around the studios in Manchester, constantly asking him how he could get into *Dad's Army*.

> There were always amusing stories about air raid wardens during the war – some of the stories may have been based on truth!
> A warden was out on duty during an air raid and saw a light on in an upstairs room. He shouted up, 'I can see a chink in your bedroom'. A lady put her head out of the window and said 'He's not a chink. He's a Japanese gentleman'.

Arthur eventually told Don to write to David Croft, which he did. David, who was always on the look-out for a character, asked Don to come down to London for an interview. The result was a small part as a removal man in 'Big Guns'.

This was Don's first speaking part in television, but he learned quickly, although the dialogue bothered him slightly in those early days. He appeared in several other episodes, including 'The Test' and 'Under Fire'.

Don Estelle who appeared in several episodes of *Dad's Army* **but who became famous as Lofty in** *It aint 'alf 'ot Mum!*. **He went on to have a hit record with Windsor Davies with the song** *Whispering Grass*.

In 1972 Don was cast as Lofty in the new series of *It aint 'alf 'ot Mum!* and Don's acting career really began in earnest. His television appearances affected his cabaret club dates in the North; he was able to ask for more money for his singing spots, which had always satisfied his audiences, and his biggest break came when he combined with the Sergeant Major (Windsor Davies) in *It aint 'alf 'ot Mum!* to record an old favourite 'Whispering Grass'. This record went to number one in the Hit Parade and brought not only more fame to Don

and Windsor but also added to the growing popularity of the television series.

Don now has his own music publishing company and writes and records his own songs.

Of his days in *Dad's Army*, he says that he was always very grateful for the help he received from everyone and that he will never forget the social occasions that sometimes accompanied the filming sessions in Norfolk. Don said with sincerity: 'I am only one of many performers who should be grateful to David Croft and Jimmy Perry for giving us a career that otherwise would probably never have happened and just left us scratching a living where we could.'

Jack Haig

Jack Haig, who plays Leclerc (the clerk) in the tremendously successful television series *'Allo 'allo*, featured in several episodes of *Dad's Army*, including 'The Day the Balloon Went Up' in which he appeared as a hedge-cutting gardener, and in another as a publican who is faced by a group of German soldiers – in actual fact they were Mainwaring's 'boys' in disguise. As usual this led to hilarious complications when Jack contacted the police with the news that 'the Germans have landed'.

Born of parents who had a very successful music hall comedy double act known as Haig and Escot, Jack like his parents, had played every variety house in the country, excluding the London Palladium. That omission has now been rectified for the former comedian and dancer with a record-breaking season as part of the stage production of *'Allo 'allo* at the world's premier theatre.

Jack progressed from the music hall to television via contracts with Tyne-Tees Television where he first met David Croft. Jack appeared in a very successful children's series called *Whacky Jacky* for seven years and then spent a number of years in *Crossroads*. He now plays the part of the forger for the Resistance in *'Allo 'allo*.

Nigel Hawthorne

Nigel played a tramp in an early episode of the series and no one needs reminding of his very successful career in the theatre, and in telvision particularly, as the indomitable Sir Humphrey in the hugely popular series *Yes Minister*.

Michael Knowles

Michael Knowles played Regular Army Captain Coutts in various episodes of *Dad's Army* and this undoubtedly led to his being cast as the silly Captain Ashwood in *It aint 'alf 'ot Mum!* which began its reign for BBC Television in 1972. That series ran for several years, including two stage productions.

Michael served *Dad's Army* in a very different capacity at a later date, and he was one of several actors whose television careers blossomed after working at the Palace Theatre, Watford.

Michael Knowles was so successful as Regular Army Captain Coutts that he went on to play the silly Captain Ashwood in *It aint 'alf 'ot Mum!*.

Geoffrey Lumsden

Geoffrey Lumsden was more than a welcome guest to *Dad's Army* and he was very much a part of the series. The character he played, Captain Colonel Square, was full of enthusiasm and blustering energy. Square's cry of 'Mainwaring' (pronounced 'Manewaring' as far as he was concerned) would always put a certain amount of fear into the platoon, and more often than not he would be happy to catch Mainwaring out on some point of order.

At this point the reason for the double ranking used by Square of 'Captain Colonel' should be explained. Ex-World War I officers who joined the Home Guard and were thought to be of sufficient knowledge and competence were given command of a platoon. This was the case with Square. As far as *Dad's Army* was concerned, the character was given command of the Eastgate Platoon with the rank of captain, just as Mainwaring was given command of the Westgate Platoon. In the series, Square had finished at the end of World War I with the rank of Colonel, so he decided to title himself 'Captain Colonel Square'.

The habit of repeating certain lines such as 'What's Mainwaring up to now? What's he up to now?' was very much part of Geoffrey's personal approach to a conversation. Arthur Lowe and I went out on a long tour in 1978 in one of Geoffrey's plays, *Caught Napping*, and there was a character of a Major General in the play which Geoffrey himself had played several years before in the West End, and this character was always repeating his lines just as Square did in the series, with very amusing results.

One had to have a sense of the ridiculous to write a play like *Caught Napping* and we, the cast, really enjoyed every moment of that tour. One of the many wonderful comic moments in the play is when the dotty butler announces that the Aga Khan has come to visit the house. The visitor is, in fact, a bookmaker dressed as a plumber, who bears no resemblance to the Aga Khan. After the plumber has left, the Major General, who is also rather dotty, says quite casually and as a matter of course, 'Funny, I always thought the Aga Khan was a much taller man.'

The seed for the play and the end-of-term frolics in school concerning a horse, a bath, a dotty master's butler and the Major General's hard-of-hearing wife was sown in Geoffrey's mind while he was at Repton College.

After leaving college, Geoffrey spent some time working at a colliery, but as he said later 'After nine months the output of coal fell so alarmingly I was handed my hat and a cheap tie pin from Wool-

worths. Deciding on a career in the theatre was the best thing I ever did.' His acting career started at London's Cambridge Theatre in 1933 and from then on Geoffrey was rarely out of London, except when he was working abroad in Canada, South Africa and New York, among other places. Eventually television claimed much of his time, but he was always happy

to return to the stage and one memorable experience was when he played with James Stewart in *Harvey*, the story of an invisible rabbit at the Prince of Wales Theatre. An actor of the old school, Geoffrey was a most convivial person. Whether he was filming or having a drink at the end of the day, he always had a story to tell about people he had known or worked with during his long career. The theatrical world was deprived of a talented actor when Geoffrey died a few years ago.

Fulton Mackay

This fine, talen ed Scottish actor featured in more than one episode of the series. Fulton's wealth of experience was apparent in his performances, not only in *Dad's Army* but in

A scene from the episode 'Battle of the Giants'. At the bar (from left to right) are Geoffrey Lumsden, Robert Raglan and Arthur Lowe. *(BBC Enterprises)*

Previous page:

Philip Madoc (right) as the commander of a German U-boat captured by the Home Guard in 'The Deadly Attachment'. *(BBC Enterprises)*

many television plays. Millions of viewers saw him as prison officer 'McCoy' in the long-running comedy series *Porridge*. Theatre audiences had always known of his talents and with a similar acting background to John Laurie, they had plenty to talk about during the filming sessions at Thetford.

colonel to keep the prisoners in the church hall for the night and to give them some food: 'Send out for some fish and chips if you haven't any food in the hall.' This led to the hilarious scene in which Private Walker was ordered to go to the fish and chip shop. Walker had to take the orders for the prisoners' meals and the U-boat Commander said that he wanted plaice and nothing else. Walker said, 'Right, I've got seven cod and one plaice so far.' He then asked who wanted chips and who wanted vinegar, etc. The commander replied that he wanted nice crispy chips, not soggy ones. Mainwaring suddenly realised that the situation was getting out of hand and said 'You'll have what you're given. If I say you'll eat soggy chips, you'll eat soggy chips.' The air raid warden then entered and completely confused the situation as he always did. The performance of Philip Madoc was a lesson in underplaying, which made the character of the German U-boat commander even more sinister.

Fulton Mackay (left) with John Laurie in 'The Miser's Hoard'. *(BBC)*

Philip Madoc

Philip appeared in the very funny episode 'The Deadly Attachment'. It was a wonderful piece of situation comedy. A German U-boat had sunk and the crew, including its commander (Philip Madoc), was drifting towards the coast at Walmington-on-Sea in a rubber dinghy. Eventually they were captured by Mainwaring and 'our gallant boys' and marched under armed guard to the church hall to await a full military escort to a secure prisoner-of-war camp. It should have been a straight-forward operation, until, that is, the air raid warden started to interfere. Mainwaring was told by his commanding

William Moore

Anyone who described one of his performances as similar to a frantic ferret, which was how William Moore thought of himself in the episode entitled 'The Royal Train', must be able to make people laugh. We had a great deal of fun filming that episode at Sheringham and Weybourne stations on the North Norfolk Railway. William who lived near me at that time, was my driving companion on a sunny Sunday journey up to Cromer where we were scheduled to stay for that filming session. We stayed at the Grand Hotel and at the time the hotel was in the hands of the receivers and the BBC had to advance them some money to buy the next day's food. I remember the jolly Irish barman saying to us 'The more you drink tonight, gentlemen, the bigger the breakfasts in the morning.' With a number of thirsty BBC actors and technicians staying at the hotel, the breakfasts were, in fact quite substantial.

The filming of this famous episode required a considerable amount of physical effort and William's idea of the frantic ferret originated from all the activity. William's part as the station master required that he should dash about, checking with the signal-box and making sure the station was spick and span, etc. As is usually the case, however the person who thinks he's in charge generally is not and expends a lot of wasted energy.

More recently, William's television appearances as Ronnie Corbett's father in *Sorry!* with his catch-phrase 'Language, Timothy' have been of a more staid and calmer character. He has enjoyed a very varied career in television, which has included two years in *Coronation Street* as Police Sergeant Turpin and in a thirteen-part series of Charles Dickens' *Dombey and Son*.

Before the long-running series *Sorry!*, William's theatrical roots were in the theatre, as is the case with many actors who have succeeded in the medium of the small screen. Trained as an engineering draughtsman, he would probably have stayed in that profession had he not had an inclination to get involved in amateur dramatics in his home town of Birmingham. Transition to professional acting was not difficult because the old and famous Birmingham Repertory Company used amateurs in the crowd scenes of some of their large-scale productions and William so enjoyed the occasions he worked for them that he decided the theatre was where

his future lay. Before long he had made his mark as a professional. He won an award for his performance in *Great Expectations* and then took part in the Pitlochry Festival in Scotland for a number of seasons where he played and directed. Teaching at the Bristol Old Vic Theatre School was another departure for this jolly and talented actor.

William related an amusing story of an event that happened when he was in J.B. Priestley's comedy *When We Are Married* at the Strand Theatre in London. Fred Emney, that larger-than-life cigar-smoking actor, was playing the photographer and J.B. Priestley himself came to watch the final dress-rehearsal. At the end of the rehearsal one of the cast said, 'He didn't laugh', referring to the playwright, and Fred Emney said, 'If he didn't think it was funny he shouldn't have written the bloody thing.'

William, who is married to actress Mollie Sugden, is a great family man, and they are proud of their twin sons who have very responsible jobs in their own particular professions.

William Moore, another fine comedy actor who made a guest appearance in *Dad's Army* **before moving on to the successful BBC series** *Sorry!* **William is married to actress Mollie Sugden.**

Gordon Peters

Gordon played the part of the fireman in a scene that was recorded but never televised. In the very first episode of the series there was a scene that involved a fireman who in true Chaplinesque fashion became tangled up in his hoses and got in everyone's way. The episode was already over running-time in rehearsals and the fireman's scene had to be edited out of the transmission. Gordon returned in several episodes, but not as a fireman. He eventually had his own series of six programmes for BBC TV and over the years has guested in several other series. He is also familiar with pantomime and cabaret, and more recently he has toured with his one-man show *Jesters*.

Robert Raglan

Bob Raglan, who played the colonel in charge of the Counties Home Guard in many episodes, was a very affable man. His own character came across in his portrayal of the colonel who had to deal with all the various eccentrics who made up the platoons under his command. Although his patience was sorely tried at times, his job was to try to keep everyone happy and not to dampen their enthusiasm, which occasionally tended to get out of hand, while at the same time maintaining some semblance of army discipline. Robert was a fine stage and film actor, but he also had just the right technique for the small screen to make any character he played very believable.

Wendy Richard

Anyone who remembers a chart-topping pop-song called 'Come Outside' might also remember that the singer was Mike Sarne and the girl who answered his invitation in the negative was Wendy Richard.

Wendy has come a long way since the recording of 'Come Outside'. Her appearances in *Dad's Army* were numerous, as she played Private Walker's girl-friend. Wendy's memories of the series are happy ones and she recalls always feeling welcome at rehearsals. I know we all loved having guests in the programme. As some folks used to say, it makes a change from listening to a lot of old buffers yackity yacking to one another.

Television viewers will be aware of Wendy's appearances in *Are You Being Served?* and *Eastenders*, but her many other television appearances include *Dixon of Dock Green, Z Cars, Up Pompeii, On the Buses, Please Sir, No Hiding Place* and *Danger Man*. She has also been a guest on almost every quiz or game show on television. Several film appearances include the *Carry On* productions, *Doctor in Clover* and *No Blades of Grass*.

Wendy was trained at the famous Italia Conti stage school after completing her general schooling at the Royal Masonic at Rickmansworth. She is a very friendly person to know and talks about her love of Chinese, Japanese and Italian food and is a good cook herself. I must say one of her hobbies worries me a bit, collecting frogs; she also collects clowns and pierrots.

Wendy has appeared in several pantomimes and in stage versions of well-known television productions. I look forward to going to one of her first nights. I know I'll be offered a glass of her favourite beverage afterwards, champagne!

Wendy Richard made numerous appearance in *Dad's Army* **and later became one of Britain's most popular television actresses with her performances in** *Are You Being Served?* **and** *Eastenders.*

Carmen Silvera

Carmen prominently featured in the episode entitled 'Mum's Army'. She and Captain Mainwaring struck up a friendship which developed into a brief encounter. This brought out the worst in the gossipy Private Fraser and one or two other members of the platoon, and rumour of a romance between them was rife in Walmington while it lasted. As usual the molehill had become a mountain in no time at all. This was one of several episodes that had pathos as well as the usual content of comedy. One of the strengths of the *Dad's Army* scripts was that the situation and ideas were consistently varied.

Carmen has worked with David Croft for many years, particularly on the very popular series *'Allo 'allo* which has firmly established her in situation comedy, although her range of acting goes very much deeper. She appeared in *Compact,* one of television's first soap operas, which was set in the publishing offices of a woman's magazine, and also acted in a fine BBC 2 drama series based on the events of World War II in Italy, although the series was filmed in Yugoslavia.

Carmen was born in Canada, her mother being Canadian. Her father was born in Jamaica and ran his own rum distillery and banana plantation on the island. The family then moved to England and Carmen became fascinated with the idea of going on the stage. She enrolled at a dancing school near Leamington Spa and by the time she was eleven had passed all the major dancing examinations. During World War II, she was evacuated to Montreal and was given her first chance to join a professional ballet company in that city.

The actress Carmen Silvera featured in the episode 'Mum's Army' where she had a 'brief encounter' with Captain Mainwaring.

After the war, by which time Carmen had returned to England, she went to drama school and was so enthusiastic and hard working that in one day she sat and obtained the bronze, silver and gold medals for the London Academy of Music and Dramatic Art.

Carmen's theatre experience includes twice-nightly repertory seasons with Harry Hanson's Court Players and Scotland's Pitlochry Festival. For five years she was assistant director at the Thorndike Theatre in Leatherhead under Hazel Vincent Wallace. Carmen was also casting director at the Thorndike and has continued her association with that theatre as a Patron.

Freddie Trueman

As most of the cast were cricket fans, it was a great thrill when we opened our scripts for the episode entitled 'The Test' and found among the extra characters was E.C. Egan, to be played by Freddie Trueman, one of England's great fast bowlers. Fred arrived in Thetford for the

A very special guest star; former England fast bowler, Freddie Trueman, enjoys a cup of tea in 'The Test'. *(Michael Fresco)*

exterior sequences on one of the very few rainy days we encountered. The character E.C. Egan had been engaged by the air raid wardens to play in the challenge match against Mainwaring's Home Guard unit; he was their secret weapon. The match was played and filmed on a disused army sports field, complete with pavilion. Although the ground was rough, Freddie made the ball come through at an alarming rate and we all felt that we were lucky not having to face him in his heyday. During his career he had been the first bowler ever to have taken three hundred Test Match wickets.

During his stay with us at Thetford the cast were invited to the Colman's Mustard head office in Norwich for a social evening and presentation of prizes to their staff. A coach was laid on to take us the thirty miles or so after a day's filming. Plenty of drinks were available as Colman's were promoting their wines from a bottling plant they had taken under their umbrella of companies. On the return journey to Thetford in the coach, Don

Estelle, who was also in the episode, Freddie and Arthur Lowe led the cast as they sang bawdy North Country songs. What with the motion of the coach, a certain amount of alcohol, and a general atmosphere of abandon, most people finished up on the floor with Don Estelle at the bottom of the pile but still singing, mostly a rude version of 'Goodbye' from White Horse Inn.

As we had been filming out in the open all day we were all in need of a square meal, and just as we came into the small town of Attleborough Arthur Lowe let out a shout of 'Stop the coach!'. He had spotted a fish and chip shop. Several of us got out of the coach and proceeded to fill the little shop that was manned by one gentleman who was guarding a solitary piece of fried cod. Arthur Lowe immediately took charge in typical Mainwaring fashion and said to the slightly astonished proprietor, 'Thirty-five portions of cod and chips, please.' Faced with the entire cast of what was by then a popular television series and with an English fast bowler of no mean reputation in Freddie Trueman, confronting him, the look on the face of the owner of the shop was, to say the least, a picture. He somehow managed to find enough fish to fulfil our order and his wife was called from her sitting-room at 10.30pm to chop up pounds of potatoes ready for the boiling fat. I'm sure the event must have been a talking point in that little Norfolk town for several months.

In 1976 when we were at the Alhambra Theatre in Bradford, on tour with the stage version of *Dad's Army*, Freddie and his wife Veronica came to see the show and invited John Le Mesurier and myself to spend the day with them at their lovely Yorkshire home. It was a day for talking cricket and viewing Fred's mementos from cricket grounds all around the world. You feel it is a privilege to be in Yorkshire when you talk to Fred Trueman, one of the proudest 'tykes' to put on a pair of cricket boots.

Edward Underdown

This tall elegant actor was cast as a staff officer in a few episodes of the series and it was a pleasure to welcome this gentle man of stage and films who had been so popular during the Forties and Fifties. Edward starred above the title in the film *The Rocking-Horse Winner* and the beginnings of his stage career went back even further when he played in several of Noel Coward's stage successes in the Thirties. An extraordinary coincidence that occurred in *Dad's Army* centred on Edward. Some of the filming for the first episode in Norfolk took place among some stables that belonged to a country house within the Stanford battle area which was by then War Department property. Nothing was left of the house except a large patio and verandah, and the stables. As soon as the cast and crew arrived at this venue John Le Mesurier realised that it was familiar to him and said, 'I used to come here for weekend parties in the Thirties when it was all private property and the house belonged to Edward Underdown's parents.' So it was that Edward found himself working in a television series that had featured part of his old home. In recent years he has worked as a steward at Newbury Race Course, which is very fitting for a man who not only loved horses but was also an expert rider. John Le Mesurier and I visited him on several occasions at his delightful cottage in the Berkshire countryside.

'To get his air raid wardens used to wearing gas masks, the chief officer of the City of London has a daily game of cricket in respirators. 'It was hard going at first but now the men are playing easily in the masks – *Daily Mirror, May 28th 1941.*

Members of the Senior Citizens Club, Thetford, used as extras in filming sequences. *(David Croft)*

Don Estelle (left) making a guest appearance in 'The Test' with Edward Sinclair and Arthur Lowe, the Verger and Captain Mainwaring. *(Gladys Sinclair)*

Croft's Weather

The Bell Hotel, Thetford. *(Boughton, Thetford)*

When we went up to Thetford for our annual filming sessions for the series we would tell our friends and relations beforehand to book their holidays at the same time. In nine years of filming in Norfolk we only had three or four days of bad weather, which included one day of snow. So the sunny days and weeks became known as Croft's weather.

It was always a joyous occasion to make the journey to Thetford where we were based for the exterior work of the series. A coach was laid on at the BBC Television Centre in Wood Lane, London, to accommodate anyone who was not going up under their own steam. A number of the cast took their own cars and a few went by train (from Liverpool Street station, changing at Ely). The wardrobe girls and boys, make-up assistants, most of the extras and two or three principals usually travelled by coach. The rest of us took our own vehicles, except John Le Mesurier who travelled with Clive Dunn or myself. Everyone took their time, generally leaving on Sunday morning and stopping for lunch on the way. Often we would pass each other en route and sometimes stop and have a chat on a country road to admire the lovely scenery, and exchange pleasantries. The production crew – cameramen, lighting and sound technicians, and the special effects department would all have gone on earlier. The gathering of the cast and crew at the hotel in Thetford was a noisy bustling affair. The wardrobe department had to get the costumes out of the caravans that had previously arrived from London, towed by Land-Rovers. A room was set aside at the hotel for the use of the wardrobe depart-

ment and the make-up girls. The hotel reception area seemed to be full of bodies: actors asking questions, sorting out their room numbers, ordering hot buttered toast to accompany the tea which they could make in their rooms. Frank Williams (the vicar) was usually enquiring whether Teddy (the verger) had brought everything out of the

The Anchor Hotel, Thetford. *(Studio Five, Thetford)*

Jones: 'Take no notice of him, Captain Mainwaring, the Verger's a spy working for Captain Square'
L to R: The author/ Warden Hodges; John Laurie/Private Fraser; Frank Williams/The Vicar; Clive Dunn/Corporal Jones; Arthur Lowe/ Captain Mainwaring; Edward Sinclair/The Verger; John Le Mesurier/Sgt. Wilson 'Battle of the Giants' *(BBC)*

car, while Frank was sorting out volumes of books and suitcases and other impedimentia he had packed into Teddy's car for the journey from London. Arthur Lowe would immediately enquire if the 'cornershop' still sold Cravan 'A' cigarettes, as that was the only brand he and his wife Joan smoked. Jimmy Perry would be telling everybody that he had brought his well-worn medicine chest with him, which included indigestion tablets, Aspro, throat spray, senna pods, diarrhoea tablets, malaria pills, snake bite ointment, shark poison antidote and a selection of plasters, splints, and spare sets of false teeth should they be needed by anyone. Other people would ask if their rooms overlooked the river, because they did not want to face the courtyard as they did last time because it was very noisy at night. With a general chorus of 'See you in the bar before dinner' the eager actors

mounted the stairs brandishing their room keys, while the girls behind the reception desk breathed a sigh of relief. However, they would quickly receive calls from various rooms with complaints of minor inconveniences.

Early on in the series, before the Bell Hotel had tea-making facilities in the rooms, Arthur Lowe would come out on to the landing early in the morning and ask 'Where's the tea-boy? He's put two tea-bags in my pot again and he knows I only have one.' The Bell was the main dormitory for the principal actors and guest artistes, and the Anchor Hotel, which was just across the river, the secondary accommodation. Both hotels had to cope with many early morning breakfasts and in some cases at the Bell serve it in the rooms, as actors would be going to the make-up girls in their tee-shirts and trousers, and only completing their wardrobe call after breakfast.

Those of us in the dining-room would discuss the news of the day or what scenes we would be filming. Arthur Lowe was generally in deep conversation with the waiter, telling him how he wanted his kippers cooked or sometimes asking if the cold ham was tender. Suddenly a production assistant would announce that the coach was leaving in five minutes, and, in an instant, actors and crew from both hotels would be congregating in the reception area of the Bell with their equipment, newspapers and other possessions waiting to start the day.

It was the job of the production assistant to make sure that everyone got on to the coach for the drive to the location. Those who were not needed for a few hours would be told to relax and that the coach or a unit car would be back to pick them up later. Getting everybody on to the coach was a military operation in itself. Someone had gener-

ally forgotten something – for example, a pair of boots they thought the dressers had but now remembered they had left them in their room, or a spare tee-shirt they wanted to change into at lunchtime.

The early morning drives out to the Stanford battle area were always sunny and we would see all sorts of wildlife, including a few dozen rabbits looking up from the grass verges, obviously saying to themselves 'what's that silly old bus doing waking us up this early'. The freshness of the dew-covered grass and the scene of the pine needles was quite exhilarating.

Once we had arrived at our destination, which would be marked by the earlier arrival of the wardrobe van, catering bus and the all-important honey wagon (toilets), not to mention various cars, technical equipment and even, if necessary, Jones' butcher's van and period vehicles of all descriptions. David Croft, who

'Get up Pike, you stupid boy!' A scene from 'We Know Our Onions'. *(Michael Fresco)*

Harold Snoad.

had bought a house nearby, had already arrived in his car and was in the process of looking for the right spot to set up the cameras and equipment for the first shot of the day. It is worth mentioning that the whole of the Stanford battle area had once consisted of small estates that were generally made up of the main house of the local gentry with perhaps a small farm, and a general stores, pub and, in some cases, their own church. This is now, and has been for a long time, War Department property, and nearly all the buildings had been used for army exercises in which battle conditions were simulated with live ammunition, so very little was left of them. Harold Snoad was the first production assistant on the series and it was he who found and selected the battle area as the main location for the exterior

'He's pinched my uniform, Captain Mainwaring'; an episode from 'Don't Forget the Diver'. *(BBC)*

filming. He explained some of the filming techniques as follows:

❝The Stanford Practical Training Area was a large area of countryside of several square miles, used by the Ministry of Defence for training our own and NATO forces. I had a very simple arrangement with the Army officer commanding the area (Colonel Cleasby-Thomson). I gave him a schedule showing where we wanted to film each day and he kept any troop training away from us. However, I do remember one occasion when things went slightly wrong. We were at a stables (disused but it still looked OK) filming a complicated sequence with the platoon trying to learn how to ride (Captain Mainwaring had decided that with strict petrol rationing the platoon's transport would be equestrian) when suddenly there was a rustle in the bushes alongside our camera and a young officer in full camouflage uniform (blackened face, the lot) politely informed me that he and his men had orders

'Man Hunt'.
(Bill Pertwee)

Pike: 'Captain Mainwaring, I'm drowning!'
Mainwaring: 'Stop whining Pike and get hold of this'
L to R: Clive Dunn/ Corporal Jones; James Beck/Private Walker; Arthur Lowe/Captain Mainwaring (back to camera) and Ian Lavender/Private Pike in 'The Big Parade' *(BBC)*

to blow up this area in ten minutes! At this a large degree of frenzied conversation ensued and, after I had made an urgent telephone call to the authorities, it was agreed, with only three minutes to go, that they would come back and blow it up the next day! I also remember we once had to film a sequence on the battle area involving Pike falling into a bog. To achieve this under controlled conditions consistent with an artiste's safety, I arranged for some soldiers to dig a pit seven feet by five and six feet deep alongside a river which ran through the area, and which one could flood slightly by dropping some sluice-gates. We did this, allowing the pit to fill up and also giving us about an inch of water over

the surrounding terrain. Once we had floated some cork chips and peat on the surface our 'bog' was just what David wanted.

We started by putting some rostra in the bottom of the pit and then, as Pike was supposed to be sinking deeper and deeper, (while Mainwaring and the rest of the platoon performed fruitless attempts to try and rescue him) we gradually reduced the height of the rostrum, allowing Pike to sink lower and lower, but we'd reduced it a bit too quickly and suddenly poor Ian Lavender was standing on tip-toe on the bottom of the pit with water up to his neck. Then the hapless Private Pike let out a terrible yell and screamed hysterically asking to be pulled out. When we had done as he had bid, we discovered that a large frog had somehow worked its way up his trouser leg. We all thought it was very funny, but Ian didn't find it quite so amusing.

The final saga of the 'bog' sequence came that evening after we had all gone back to the Bell Hotel. I hadn't realised, but it was the habit of the helpful Army officer in charge of the battle area (the afore-mentioned Colonel Cleasby-Thomson) to walk his dog by the river every evening. He was the sort of man who wore tough knee-high boots and so thought nothing of strolling through 'puddles' alongside his river. Unfortunately he had forgotten that we had been filming the 'bog' sequence and suddenly disappeared up to his neck in dirty water. When I went to see him the next day to tell him that the 'rushes' were OK and that the hole could be filled in, he was not in quite his normal cherry mood, but I invited him and his wife to join us for dinner at the Bell Hotel that evening and all was forgiven. **9**

Some of the chase sequences that involved a lot of vehicles were very tiring for everyone concerned, and not just the actors, but the results were usually good and in the tradition of the old Mack Sennett comedies. It generally finished with Warden Hodges being flung into a lake or being pushed off a bridge into the river; on one occasion he had a mushy type of custard-coloured liquid poured over him from a great height. In this latter sequence the warden was trying to guide a spotter plane which was carrying the custard liquid over to the place where he knew Mainwaring and his men

were hiding; however, the plane dropped its load on top of Hodges by mistake. This sequence was filmed first with the aeroplane flying overhead and then dustbins full of the liquid were filmed as they were emptied from the top of a high crane to simulate aerial movement. Unfortunately, the liquid quickly went solid and filled Hodges' ears.

'I (Hodges) was taken in a fast unit car to Thetford Cottage Hospital for treatment. When we arrived, however, a notice on the gate informed us that it was half-day closing. We eventually found a doctor who dealt with the problem using various instruments and a syringe. I also needed a long soak in the bath to get the rest of the liquid off my body.'

In another episode Hodges was riding the familiar 1940s

A warden was directing people to 'get down in the shelter, there's a raid in progress'. He banged on one front door and called 'Come on down into the shelter'. An elderly voice from behind the door said 'Hold on, I'm just going upstairs to get me teeth'. The warden shouted back, 'They're dropping bombs, not bloody sandwiches!'

'Even Hitler would be frightened to meet him on a dark night': Warden Hodges

'Put that light out'

motor-bike with the vicar on the pillion and the verger in the side-car. It was a fairly fast ride into camera shot but suddenly a mechanical failure caused the machine to go out of control and the camera and sound crew had to jump for their lives. The vicar's only comment was 'I hope the verger didn't have his usual roughage for breakfast.'

On another occasion when we were filming at Lowestoft, the warden, having seen the lighthouse illuminated and guessing that Mainwaring's platoon had had something to do with it (in fact, they had been guarding it and Corporal Jones had touched the on switch), decided to row out to them. He cut loose a pedallo boat which had been tied up on the beach at the outbreak of war and paddled towards the lighthouse. He didn't know that the boats had been holed to stop them being used by an enemy landing force. The idea for the film sequence was that the warden should get halfway to his objective and then slowly sink. David Croft and the camera crew were on the jetty, filming the action. Suddenly, an enveloping mist descended and nothing was visible – the camera crew, Hodges in the boat or the shore. The only sound– and it was an eerie sound at 2 o'clock in the morning – was of the sirens of fishing-boats that were trying to find the harbour. Luckily, Hodges, who was far out to sea by now, was picked up by a diver and

The Verger and the Warden in trouble again in 'Gorilla Warfare'.
(Brian Fisher)

Above: **The Warden in the drink again.** *(Bill Pertwee)*

'Who does he think he's kidding, Mr. Hitler?'. The Warden in 'Two and a Half Feathers'. *(Bill Pertwee)*

guided in to the shore. Harold Snoad was on hand to administer large doses of Scotch and to get the luckless Hodges back to the hotel in Yarmouth.

Very early the next morning Warden Hodges was rehearsing the boat scene again off the Britannia pier. Although the water looked very calm from high up on the pier, when the warden was put into the water wearing only his helmet and a flesh-coloured jockstrap, the waves knocked him back on to the girders beneath. The scene required that Hodges should be chased by a sea mine that was attracted to his steel helmet. It was quickly decided to use a stunt double for the scene, and Hodges had only to fall in the water – although it was very cold!

The warden was also in some peril during the 'Royal Train' episode. The mayor of Walmington, the vicar, the verger and warden were crowded on to a pump truck trying to stop a runaway railway engine that was carrying Mainwaring and his lads. The pump truck is like a small platform with two levers which, when hand pumped,

Setting up for the filming of 'The Royal Train' at Weybourne Station. *(Brian Fisher)*

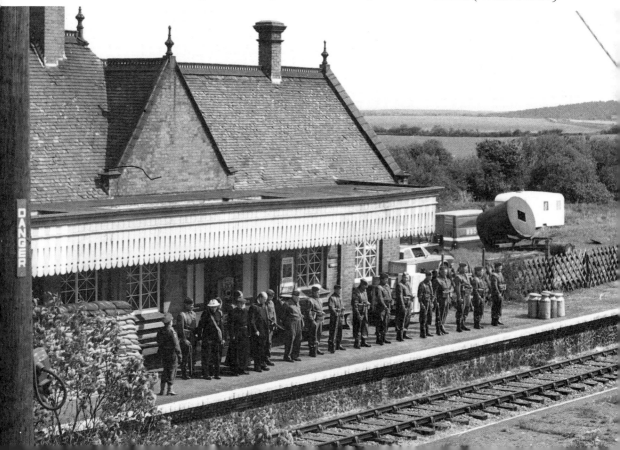

simply propel it along. The truck was in a small cutting and going very fast in pursuit of the engine when one of the handles caught in the warden's trouser pocket, tore it and began to lift the warden up in the air. He managed to save himself, but he could easily have gone over the side. The cast of the platoon also had to take care because most of them were crawling about on the engine complete with camera crew.

Clive Dunn had some hair-raising sequences to do as Corporal Jones. On one occasion he had to climb out on to the town hall roof and try to pull in a German pilot who had bailed out of his aircraft and been caught on the hands of the town hall·clock. Some of

A famous scene: chasing 'The Royal Train'. (*Brian Fisher*)

this was done with trick photography, but the final result was excellent. Harold Snoad recounts another Jones escapade:

❛The sequence called for Corporal Jones to get caught up on the sails of a large windmill and fly round several times on same. We found a huge windmill which looked very impressive, but of course it only went round if there was almost a gale force wind (unlike some others it hadn't been converted to other 'turning' systems). As we couldn't possibly film in those conditions I suddenly hit upon the idea of putting what looked like a small timber hut on the ground between the camera and the sails of the windmill. In fact the hut didn't have a back and two strong scene boys stood behind it and once we'd got it going they kept the sails turning by giving each of them a shove as the bottom end came past them. It worked extremely well.❜

Another difficult episode to make was entitled 'The Day the Balloon Went Up'. The story revolved around a barrage balloon that had broken loose from its moorings and was hovering above the church hall. Mainwaring organised everybody, even the reluctant Warden Hodges, to take the guy ropes and to walk the balloon into open country and to wait for the Army to come and pick it up. In the exterior filming sequences, the whole platoon, plus the warden, vicar and verger, are seen holding the ropes. Captain Mainwaring managed to

A break during the filming of 'Don't Forget the Diver'. *(BBC)*

'The Day the Balloon went up'. *(Bill Pertwee)*

get his legs caught up in one of the ropes and he goes up with the balloon as it rises when the others panic and let go of their ropes. The journey of Mainwaring skimming over the tree-tops (in fact, a stunt-man was on the end of the rope) was quite hilarious, and the final scene in which he is caught under a railway bridge in the path of an approaching train before he is rescued by the rest of the platoon, was in the best traditions of screen comedy.

Much of the filming was done in Thetford itself and this gave us all a chance to get to know the people of this little Norfolk town. Jean Bishop, who owned the Anchor Hotel at that time, became a real friend to us all and made us feel most wel-come when we met there for dinner or a drink before eating at the Bell. Jean threw a few parties for us and was a good hostess. The staff at the Bell Hotel were most helpful and always made sure we were well looked after. In the early days, the rushes (rough cut) of the day's filming would be put on the train to London and returned next day for us to see. These we viewed at the

Relaxing in the bar with Jean Bishop, who was then the owner of the Anchor Hotel, Thetford.

little local cinema in Thetford after the regular film show finished at night. At 10.30 pm, a group of actors could be seen walking up the road to the cinema and waiting for the 'late' doors to open. Sequences of the filming were greeted with 'Look at the warden, over-acting again' or 'So and so could have done better then'. A funny sequence would be greeted with spasmodic applause or laughter. Arthur Lowe would generally fall asleep but wake up at just the right moment to make a cryptic remark. We would then return to our respective hotels for a night-cap or two. Harold Snoad continues:

❛Whenever we had to do any filming in the streets of Thetford it was necessary for the windows of any houses we saw in the background (and this could be quite a large number in some of the platoon marching sequences) to look correct – ie criss-crossed with brown sticky tape as they would have been during the war. When we first started filming the series we used to spend many a long hour trudging up the road visiting each house with rolls of sticky tape, explaining what we wanted and often having to do the job ourselves. We very quickly decided that this was far too time-consuming, so when the second series came along we duplicated copies of a letter explaining what we wanted, with a diagram of a typical finished window, and these were dropped through their letter boxes in envelopes along with a roll of brown sticky tape and a pound note for their trouble. And everybody obliged!❜

Above: **'I say, steady on, I don't even know your name'; Wilson is embarrassed by this demonstration of the entente cordiale in 'The Captain's Car'.** *(BBC)*

Below: **Our heroes trying to frighten the townsfolk out of their complacency in 'Wake Up Walmington'.** *(BBC)*

Above: **Captain Mainwaring's nightmare as Napoleon in 'A Soldier's Farewell'.** *(BBC)*
Below: **'Everybody's trucking'.** *(BBC Enterprises)*

There were certainly some magic moments that I shall never forget. Several old vehicles were lined up in the street one day ready for filming when a traffic warden appeared and told David Croft that he couldn't park the vehicles on a yellow line. David explained that we were filming and would be as quick as possible. The traffic warden looked at one of the old vehicles – an Austin Seven – and said 'And by the way, the tax disc is out of date; it's showing 1940.'

At breakfast one morning at the hotel, we learned from the newspaper that Clive Dunn had been awarded an OBE. Clive was already in make-up and we would not be able to see him until we got on the coach. Arthur Lowe was tucking into his breakfast and someone asked him what he thought about Clive being awarded an OBE. Arthur looked up, put down his knife and fork, adjusted his glasses and said, 'Very good, but when it comes to my turn I don't want any of that bargain basement stuff.' I hope I'm not speaking out of turn when I say that I think Arthur was overdue for some recognition at the end of the series.

John Le Mesurier always amused me. On one occasion he said to me, 'I don't want to eat in the hotel tonight, let's go and get some fish and chips.' So we drove out of Thetford and found a fish and chip

'We do like dressing up'; 'Knights of Madness'. *(Bill Pertwee)*

shop. I told him that we couldn't eat them in the car as they would leave a terrible smell. We drove on until we found a bus shelter on a lonely stretch of road. Sitting in the shelter eating our fish and chips in the fading light of the evening, John turned to me and said, 'Our programme's watched by twenty million people. Such is fame, if only the public could see us now, up to our elbows in batter in a bus shelter in Norfolk.'

Harold Snoad remembers an instance when we were filming on a very hot day and John looked at his watch and found that it had stopped. He said, 'This heat is really exhausting. Could someone wind up my watch for me, please?'

Harold Snoad knew exactly what David Croft wanted in the way of filming sequences, etc and was obviously destined to go further within the BBC. This he has done as the producer/director of some of their top comedy programmes such as *The Dick Emery Show, Don't Wait Up, Ever Decreasing Circles* and *Brush Strokes.*

The social highlight of our stay in Thetford was a visit, sometimes more than one, to David and Ann's house for a large Sunday lunch. All the children, from toddlers to teenagers, were there and also

Ann's parents who lived in a bungalow that had been converted from a part of the main farmhouse. David and Ann were the ideal hosts and the table would groan under the weight of the food and wine, all of which was accompanied by great conviviality. We swam in the pool, played cricket with the youngsters, watched the girls riding their ponies around the field and chatted to one or two local villagers who had come in to help Ann make it an enjoyable occasion for us. We, of course, tried to reciprocate by inviting David and Ann to dinner with us at the Bell when they were free to do so, but it was a poor return for the wonderful times we spent under their roof.

Saying goodbye to Thetford for another year was always tinged with sadness for we had become attached to it over the years. We hoped that the filming that had been achieved would be appreciated by the studio audience in London when they saw it cut into the scenes we would be recording a few weeks later.

I asked Arthur Lowe a few years after we had finished making the series whether he would like to return to Thetford and he replied, 'No, it holds too many ghosts for me' – and I know what he meant.

'Mainwaring's gone too far this time'; scene from 'Battle of the Giants'.
(Bill Pertwee)

Film Stars

The Columbia Pictures feature film of *Dad's Army* was made early in the show's career in 1970 and was premiered in March 1971.

One of the locations for the film was Chalfont St Peter in Buckinghamshire. This pretty little town was transformed into Walmington-on-Sea, complete with some small boats, fishing-nets, the Swallow Bank, Hodges' greengrocer's shop. Jones' butcher's shop, etc, all of which had only been seen in interior studio mock-ups in the television series.

Another location was Chobham in Surrey, where two hair-raising scenes occurred, one causing John Laurie to finish up with very badly bruised ribs. There was a long scene in which a white horse had to cross the river on a raft with our heroes on board. The raft was being towed downstream by way of ropes that

'Right men, get that furniture across the road. It will stop the Hun in his tracks': a scene from the feature film.
(Columbia Pictures Industries Inc.)

DAD'S ARMY

Previous page:
**The opening shot
from the feature film
of** *Dad's Army.*
*(Columbia Pictures
Industries Inc. 1970)*

**German General
played by Paul
Dawkins in the
feature film.**
*(Columbia Pictures
Industries Inc. 1970)*

were handled from the river bank. The rather jerky movements of the tow lines unbalanced the horse and it slipped and fell, hitting John Laurie. It was not a pleasant thing to happen to anyone, let alone to someone in their seventies and an asthma sufferer as well. However, John recovered and luckily everyone else was unharmed.

Other locations that were used for filming were Seaford in Sussex, various streets around Shepperton in Middlesex, and the interior filming at Shepperton Studios.

The film was produced by John Sloan and directed by Norman Cohen. It was not an easy assignment for the director or actors. Columbia Pictures were determined to make the film on time – eight weeks was their target, although it did take a little longer. Jimmy Perry and David Croft, the writers and advisers for the production, spent a great deal of time and energy in trying to make sure that the film was kept in the Forties style. It was, of course, not so easy for an American film company to think of the era in the same way as we did. David and Jimmy and all the television crew knew the actors well, and they always ensured that they were comfortable and happy and not being hurried into their work.

The feature film was a slightly different matter. The producer constantly pressurised the director to get so many minutes in the can per day, and this in turn pressurised the production. We did

TURES Presents **DAD'S ARMY** u A NORCON PRODUCTION
R LOWE · **JOHN LE MESURIER** · **CLIVE DUNN**
LAURIE · JAMES BECK · ARNOLD RIDLEY
IAN LAVENDER · LIZ FRASER
by JIMMY PERRY and DAVID CROFT · Produced by JOHN R. SLOAN
NORMAN COHEN · TECHNICOLOR ›
advertising material is licensed and not sold and is the Property of National Screen Service Ltd. and upon
of the exhibition for which it has been licensed it should be returned to National Screen Service Ltd.

so Arthur decided to look for one himself. He ordered a unit car and, accompanied by one or two other actors, including Paul Dawkins who was playing the German general, drove from the studios to the nearest Woolworth's store. The sight of a large limousine pulling up outside Woolworth's and Arthur, plus the German general in full military uniform, caused a few raised eyebrows among the passersby. The Woolworth's staff were even more surprised at being confronted by Captain Mainwaring and a German general asking for a plastic revolver. The store couldn't help, however, and Arthur, with his uniformed entourage, left the shop muttering 'You could always buy a sixpenny pistol in Woolworth's when I was a lad.'

There were some very funny sequences in the feature film, although it didn't have the overall atmosphere of the television production. It was not an expensive film to produce and many cinema managers have been delighted financially with the business they have done with it, particularly at holiday times. All of the actors and production team associated with it have agreed that it has improved with age. The public certainly enjoys it because some of them have gone out their way to say so each time it has an airing on television, which it has had on more than one occasion.

The official London premiere of the movie took place at the Columbia Cinema in London, and we all did some publicity appearances for it at various cinemas around the Home Counties when it was on general release.

In 1970 it was just another sequence of events during the reign of *Dad's Army*, but we all had to get back to work quickly in the television studios to make more episodes for the small screen.

have some very helpful assistants among the film crew, which was a great advantage. John Le Mesurier, who was the most experienced film actor among us, knew a few of the crew from previous films in which he had acted, so that also helped.

Actors tend to find amusement in off-screen incidents and one such occasion was when Arthur Lowe was given a rather heavy and cumbersome revolver to use, without ammunition, because it didn't actually have to be fired. Arthur commented that as this was the case could not the prop department find a plastic replica which would be easier to handle and quicker to get out of the holster he was wearing. The prop department said they didn't think they could,

'Many men, having joined up themselves, did their best to bring in additional members; golf clubs, containing many retired officers, being a particularly fertile recruiting ground. At the Cobble Hall Club, near Leeds, fifty-seven golfers (of whom eighteen were ex-officers) and several ex-servicemen, formed a self-contained platoon which took over the defence of their course against the intrusion of any German non-members who might arrive without paying the usual green fee. The unit's first Standing Orders for patrols had a distinctive flavour:

Dress: Golf gear
Arms: A stout stick
Guard Room: Club lounge – easy chairs for sleep

.. Membership proved to be popular and four-man patrols would play a round of golf before setting off for work' – Norman Longmate, *The Real Dad's Army*

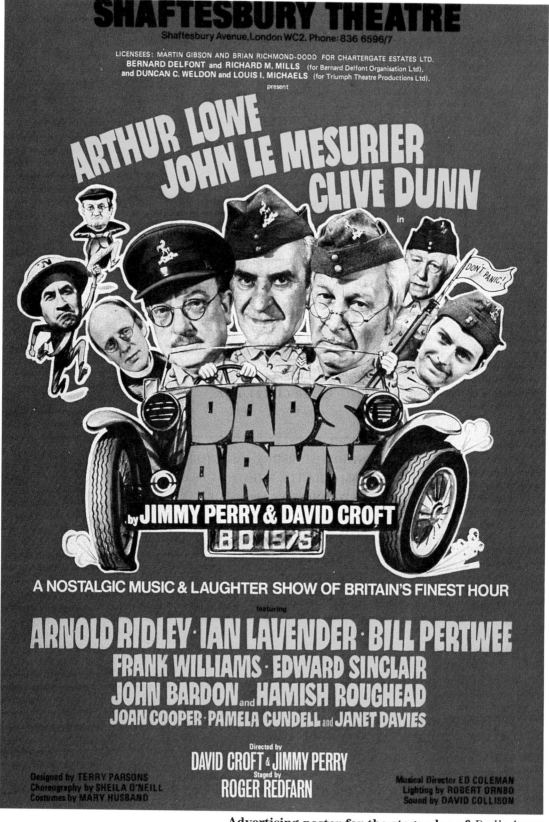

Advertising poster for the stage play of *Dad's Army.*

Treading the Boards

The stage musical of *Dad's Army* was a major event in our lives in 1975 and 1976. We had heard about it sometime before, but in no great detail. We were all asked whether we would be available and if we wanted to do it. Bernard, now

Some of the cast relaxing in Arthur Lowe's dressing room. *(Woman Magazine)*

Lord Delfont, who had already produced many large-scale musical and pantomimes, not only in London but all over the country, was to combine with Louis Michaels and Duncan Weldon of Triumph Theatre productions in presenting the stage show. The television series was popular with the public and they all thought it would be a good box office attraction. Contracts were arranged, but as yet no London theatre had been decided upon. All the principal actors would be in the show, with the exception of John Laurie, who felt that working in the theatre every night and travelling between Buckinghamshire and London every day would be too tiring for him. The show was also to include Frank Williams, Teddy Sinclair, Pam Cundell, Janet Davies and myself, all of us regular members of the television series. Replacements had to be found for John Laurie and Jimmy Beck, who had died some time before. There was no question that John or Jimmy could be replaced, but the characters had to be reproduced. It was not an easy task, particularly for the actors who would be playing the well-known characters of privates Fraser and Walker, but still be able to creat a personality of their own, which is very important on stage. The two actors who were eventually cast in theses difficult roles were John Bardon, as Walker and Hamish Roughead as Fraser.

The ideas for the script and content of the show had been discussed but not in detail, and it was while we were filming, before we had received our scripts, that Jimmy Perry informed us what the show would be about. Jimmy is a very enthusiastic person at the best of times, but when he is in a dynamic mood, perhaps charged with a glass or two of red wine, he is unstoppable. The particular evening at the Bell Hotel in Thetford when he decided to explain to a few of us what he and David had in mind was both exhilarating and funny. He asked Frank Williams, Ted Sinclair and myself to come up to his room where he could explain the details. Once Jimmy had started, he gave us a solo performance of the proposed show. He dashed about his bedroom, leapt on the bed, rushed to the door, and went in and out of the bathroom depicting various scenes. He explained how the show would open up with some film of the 1940s on a back-projection screen; he demonstrated this by mimicking Winston Churchill in front of the large mirror. He explained how Warden Hodges would make his first entrance from the audience, interrupting the verger and vicar who were singing a chanting-type song about the black-out. Private Pike would have to sing a big production number entitled 'When can I have a banana

DAD'S ARMY

ACT 1

Scene 1   Who Do You Think You Are Kidding Mr. Hitler
Scene 2   Put That Light Out
Scene 3   Carry On On The Home Front
          British Restaurant
Scene 4   Command Post
Scene 5   Private Pike's Dream
Scene 6   L/Cpl. Jones Stands Guard
Scene 7   Lords of the Air
Scene 8   Choir Practice

ACT 2

Scene 1   The Song We Would Rather Forget
Scene 2   Unarmed Combat
Scene 3   Tin Pan Alley Goes to War
Scene 4   A Nightingale Sang in Berkeley Square
Scene 5   Morris Dance
Scene 6   Radio Personalities of 1940
Scene 7   The Beach
Scene 8   Finale

There will be an interval of fifteen min
between Act One and Act Two

SHAFTESBURY THEATRE
Shaftesbury Avenue London WC2   01-836 6596/7
LICENSEES: MARTIN GIBSON & BRYAN RICHMOND-DODD
for CHARTERGATE ESTATES LTD.
THEATRE MANAGEMENT: RICHARD SCHULMAN

BERNARD DELFONT and RICHARD M. MILLS
(for Bernard Delfont Organisation Ltd.)
and DUNCAN C. WELDON and LOUIS I. MICHAELS
(for Triumph Theatre Productions Ltd.)

present

**ARTHUR LOWE
JOHN LE MESURIER
CLIVE DUNN**

in

DAD'S ARMY
by JIMMY PERRY and DAVID CROFT
A Nostalgic Music and Laughter Show of Britain's Finest Hour

with

**ARNOLD
RIDLEY**   **IAN
LAVENDER**   **BILL
PERTWEE**

FRANK WILLIAMS   **EDWARD SINCLAIR**
JOHN BARDON and **HAMISH ROUGHEAD**
JOAN COOPER   PAMELA CUNDELL and JAN DAVIES

Directed by
DAVID CROFT & JIMMY PERRY

Staged by
ROGER REDFARN

Designed by TERRY PARSONS   Musical Director ED COLEMAN
Musical Staging SHEILA O'NEILL   Lighting by ROBERT ORNBO
Costumes by MARY HUSBAND   Sound by DAVID COLLISON

A FORUM THEATRE BILLINGHAM PRODUCTION
First Performance at the Shaftesbury Theatre, Thursday 2nd October 1975

again?', which we were to hear a lot more of once rehearsals began. Ian (Pike) was to be zipped up in a huge plastic banana and dash about asking people when he could have the elusive banana (not seen in this country during World War II). Jimmy looked so funny leaping around his bedroom as a banana that Frank Williams laughed uncontrollably until he had to plead for Jimmy to stop. Jimmy, however, continued unabated. He then started to sing 'Follow the White Line', a song that advised people what to do when they were walking home in the black-out. This he demonstrated, taking us in tow in conga fashion around the room. And so he continued, demonstrating various acts, playing all the characters and singing all the songs until be finally sat down on his bed and said, 'Well, how does that sound?' Ted Sinclair, who had sat motionless through it all, said, 'I'm tired out and the show hasn't even started yet!.'

The first day of rehearsal for the show was at the Richmond Theatre, the lovely Victorian playhouse in Surrey. The director was a young man called Roger Redfarn who had, among other things, been artistic director at the successful Belgrade Theatre at Coventry. David Croft and Jimmy Perry were obviously going to be very much in evidence, advising, suggesting and keeping a close eye on the production. The musical director who was in charge of a large orchestra was an American, Ed Coleman. Ed proved to be a tremendous help to us as rehearsals got underway and afterwards during the actual production. For Ed cajoled, shouted, encouraged and complimented the cast, all in the space of a few minutes. On the first day of rehearsal he got the whole company together and made us sing collectively and solo the first two bars of

'Somewhere over the Rainbow'. His experience was such that he could judge our singing range with that short burst of song. The choreographer was Sheila O'Neill, who had the task of teaching people of all shapes and sizes, some with two left feet like me, and several of them new to a full stage musical, but each and everyone very enthusiastic. Also in the cast was Joan Cooper, Arthur Lowe's wife, who was to play Private Godfrey's sister Dolly, as she had done on numerous occasions in the television series, Eric Longworth who had played the town clerk in several episodes, and Michael Bevis who was to feature in one of the production numbers. Also taking part were Norman MacLeod, Bernice Adams, Debbie Blackett, Ronnie Grange, Graham Hamilton, Vivian Pearman, Peggy Ann James, Barrie Stevens, Jan Todd, David Wheldon Williams, Alan Woodhouse, Michelle Summers, June Shand, Kevin Hubbard and Jeffery Holland, who would be playing a mad German inventor as well as being part of the general production team.

Jeffrey did his audition for the show while he was playing a season at the Chichester Festival Theatre and on the recommendation of Roger Redfarn. Jeffrey was very depressed that he had been booked for only one of the plays at Chichester and not for all four plays in the repertoire as was usual. He had grown fond of that lovely city in the heart of the Sussex countryside so he was not in the best of spirits when he travelled up to London for the audition for the *Dad's Army* stage musical. Being a true professional, Jeffrey determined to do well in the audition and then to return for his last few weeks at Chichester. He had learned the song 'When can I have a banana again?' as he knew

Such was the popularity of *Dad's Army* that when we started the provincial tour of the stage show, we found it difficult even to go out together to a restaurant because all of the cast were so easily recognised. At one 'eaterie' we looked up to discover thirty people staring through the restaurant window at us, watching their TV favourites eating. As Arthur Lowe said 'I now know how the chimps feel at the zoo's tea party'. We did, of course, appreciate the wonderful public following we had!

this was going to be part of the show. He did the audition and was engaged immediately by David and Jimmy so he returned to Chichester in delight.

Jeffrey had considerable experience as an actor after he gave up an office job when he was young and decided to follow a career in the theatre. Four and a half years at the Belgrade Theatre in Coventry near his home town of Walsall and small parts in television had smoothed the rough edges, but *Dad's Army* was the turning point in his career. He later joined us for an episode in the television series as a driver of a heavy-duty service vehicle. In 1980 Jeffrey was cast by Jimmy and David as the comedian Spike in their new series *Hi-De-Hi* and from there he has never looked back. He recalls the time in his life when he went to audition for the stage musical of *Dad's Army*:

Jeffrey Holland

6 I had a marvellous year with that show. Six months in London and six months on tour. From an audition I really wasn't too bothered about I got a job that was an absolute joy and afforded me the privilege of working with a cast and a show that were then and are now a legend. Just think, if I had done the four plays at Chichester instead of just one it would never have happened, and my life and career in the theatre would almost certainly have been quite different. **9**

After three weeks rehearsal at Richmond we made our way north to Billingham, in Cleveland, for the out-of-town opening of the show. We were due to run it in at the Forum Theatre there before moving into the Shaftesbury Theatre, London, in the autumn.

The Forum is a modern, well-equipped theatre, part of an entertainments complex, with swimming-pool, squash courts, snooker etc. Les Jobson, an ex-schoolmaster, the artistic director and his staff all combined to make us very welcome. However the stage door-keeper was obviously confused about our names for when John Le Mesurier arrived, he greeted him with the words 'Good morning, Sir, are you Arnold Lowe?'.

The extensive workshops of the Forum had made all the sets, most of which were quite complicated and extra staff had to be drafted in to handle them. They were designed to represent the two sides of the English Channel and consisted of two electrically controlled trucks that moved on to the stage from the wings. Corporal Jones was on top of one truck guarding the British coast, while the German general (played by myself) and the mad inventor sat on top of the opposite truck looking out from France. On another occasion Private Godfrey would glide on stage on a truck that represented his cottage garden, talking to his sister Dolly (who was so adept at making upside-down cakes) about the current cricket scores, which to him were more important than anything else. On another truck Field Marshall Goering would be extolling the virtues of the Luftwaffe and how they were going to blast the British out of the skies. The scene finished with Godfrey reciting 'Lords of the Air' and the boys and girls forming a choir in the background. This was a very moving moment in the show and it was played superbly by Arnold Ridley and Joan Cooper. We were very lucky to have such a good company of boys and girls as a back-up to the established principals. They had been picked mainly for their singing and dancing abilities, but were

One night Jeffrey Holland was having a meal in a restaurant with Arthur Lowe and his wife Joan. Arthur asked for the wine list and after perusing it for a while said to the waitress 'Have you got a Macon?'. The waitress, without a smile, replied 'No, it's an overall'.

also to prove accomplished actors.

During the technical rehearsal there were moments of anxiety concerning such matters as whether certain equipment was going to work or whether a scene that had been envisaged on paper would prove successful in practice. One such scene was the banana production which some of us had been privy to in Jimmy's bedroom at Thetford. It was rehearsed and re-rehearsed many times. We would get to the theatre in the morning only to be told that for the next couple of hours, only the banana people were required. So some of us would simply walk around the Billingham shopping precinct. We all agreed that we would never eat another banana! The problems with the song were finally sorted out and it proved to be a big success in the show, much to Ian Lavender's relief because he had been in and out of that plastic banana skin many times over.

On other occasions some members of the company would be given the whole day off because scenes were being rehearsed that did not include them, so we would pile into a car and take a trip out on the moors for a pub lunch, or go down to the North Yorkshire coastal harbours of Staithes and Robin Hood's Bay. The beautiful scenery and friendliness of the Yorkshire people act as a tonic, and to walk into the little resort of Staithes from the car park on the hill and wander among the fishermen's cottages is a joy. Whitby is a much larger place, but is certainly worth a visit and, apart from a particular little establishment near Yorkshire's Headingly cricket ground, has the best fish and ship shops in the country, and even one or two pubs there make their fish luncheons taste like gourmet dishes.

Opening night at the Forum

was now getting very close. We were working long hours on some days and Roger Redfarn was becoming oblivious of the time of day as we went through songs, dance routines, dialogue and costume rehearsals. At two o'clock one morning I realised that the uncomplaining boys and girls had had no supper, not even a sandwich, and our strength was beginning to sag. I therefore walked on to the stage and quite out of turn, announced that everyone had obviously had enough for that night. There was a silence in which you could have heard a pin drop. Suddenly Arthur Lowe said, 'I quite agree' and that was the end of rehearsals for that night.

Apart from all the production numbers they were involved in, some of the boys

German General (the author) and mad inventor (Jeffrey Holland).
(Stuart Robinson)

DAD'S ARMY

Mainwaring: 'Now if a Nazi stormtrooper comes cycling into view, pick up the nearest chair, push the chair legs through his spokes, grab his gun and there's another Jerry in the bag, simple!'
L to R: Hamish Roughead (back to camera), Arnold Ridley, Clive Dunn, Arthur Lowe, Graham Hamilton, Norman Macleod, John Le Mesurier, Ian Lavender, Eric Longworth, John Bardon. A scene from the stage production at the Shaftesbury Theatre, London (*Stuart Robinson*)

and girls were understudying the principals and had to learn their lines as well, which was a considerable task. Eric Longworth was covering for Arthur Lowe, Michael Bevis for John Le Mesurier and Norman Macleod for Clive Dunn. Norman was one of the principal singers and had at one time been lead singer with a famous Canadian group, The Maple Leaf Four. There was a very complicated production number called 'Too Late' about the killing of General Gordon at Khartoum which featured Clive Dunn recalling Corporal Jones' experiences as a young soldier. John Le Mesurier had a scene with Private Pike and his mother, which led into 'A Nightingale Sang in Berkeley Square', sung by John. This was given all the experience of John's theatrical technique and proved to be one of those quiet but delightful moments

that you occasionally experience in the theatre.

Several of us were involved in a scene that concerned radio personalities of the Forties. Arthur Lowe did a very passable impersonation of Robb Wilton, with all the comic mannerisms of that great humourist. In fact, as I have mentioned earlier (p.26), Arthur's timing and general approach to comedy was reminiscent of Wilton.

Pam Cundell and Joan Cooper appeared as Elsie and Doris Waters (Gert and Daisy), sisters of Jack Warner (the Dixon of Dock Green policeman); three of the girls combined in a very good presentation of the American favourites the Andrews sisters; and Arthur also played Mr Lovejoy with Michael Bevis as Ramsbottom and Ian Lavender as Enoch as 'We Three in Happidrome' fame

who were a huge radio success during the war. I was given the opportunity to portray the cheeky chappie, Max Miller. I was slightly worried about performing this at Billingham, because although Miller had been a great bill topper in his heyday in variety at the London Palladium and elsewhere, he had never performed in the most northern areas of the country. I had actually worked with Max Miller when I was playing in

the other side, and so it went on with the whole cast eventually arriving on stage with those in the back rows carrying life-size cut-outs of Flanagan and Allen and all singing 'Hometown'. It was a tremendously effective scene. The only two members of the cast who were not involved in 'Hometown' were myself and Jeffery Holland; we followed high up on our truck, commenting on the uncertainies of our future now that it looked

Rehearsal of 'The Floral Dance' for the Royal Variety Performance at the London Palladium.
(Doug McKenzie)

variety in the 1950s, so I had some idea of his style and this helped considerably.

To complete the entertainment scene of the 1940s, Arthur Lowe and John Le Mesurier appeared as Flanagan and Allen, those great stars of the Crazy Gang. The song 'Hometown' started with Arthur and John walking across the stage and when they got to the other side they picked up two more members of the cast who were dressed the same way, they then walked back again and picked up two more members from

as if the Allies were going to win the war.

One of the most enjoyable pieces to perform was the Morris Dance, which involved a disciplined routine that went haywire when it was performed by Mainwaring's boys, together with the Warden who started arguing with Jones and brandishing his club, causing chaos until Mainwaring restored order. The sight of people dressed in white costumes, panama hats, bells and colourful tassels looked most attractive.

Another enjoyable piece was

the Floral Dance, a comedy routine which also involved the whole cast and which was a rehearsal for the Home Guard and citizens of Walmington of a choir concert they were going to give in aid of wounded soldiers. It not only included some wonderful visual comedy but also very funny dialogue. Both 'The Morris Dance' and 'The Choir Practice' had been adapted for the stage from the television episodes, so there was a certain amount of confidence in them

The opening night suddenly arrived and we just hoped that the packed theatre would receive the show well. We need not have worried, however, for apart from one or two minor technical hitches and overrunning a little, most people enjoyed it. It hadn't been easy for Roger Redfarn or Jimmy and David, but no matter what the directors do, everything depends on the actors and actresses once the curtain goes up.

The rest of our short stay at Billingham went well, with crowds coming in from all over the North East to see us. We had a very friendly array of dressers and stage staff, which certainly helped the overall atmosphere.

Once back in London we were to open our West End run at the Shaftesbury Theatre. Some cuts had to be made during the two or three days' rehearsal at the Shaftesbury as we were still over-running. At this time I was also asked to record a song for EMI that had been written around a phrase that I often used in the television series describing Mainwaring's mob as 'hooligans'; the reverse side was to be an oldie, 'Get Out and Get Under the Moon'. This was recorded in company with Norman Macleod from the stage show.

We had a few days of previews at the Shaftesbury and then came the official opening night. The atmosphere was electric, with a packed house that included some friends and relations, and it seemed we would stay at the London Venue for a while yet. One night at the theatre Norman Macleod recognised the former prime minister Sir Alec Douglas Home in the audience. On his way home to Brighton Norman found himself standing next to Sir Alec on the platform of the Underground station ad asked him if he had enjoyed the show. Sir Alec replied,'Very much, I'm a fan of *Dad's Army.*' Some of us had met Sir Alec previously when he was our host at a Saints and Sinners charity lunch in London. He was very kind and thoughtful on that occasion and proved to be a charming and warm person.

Very early into the run we were all asked to stay on stage after the show. We were then informed that we had been invited to take part in the annual Royal Variety performance at the London Palladium in the presence of Her Majesty the Queen and the Duke of Edinburgh. This was exciting news and it was decided that we should perform the Floral Dance choir item, as this was not only a good comedy piece which was going well at the Shaftesbury, but it also included the whole cast. We had had one or two bomb scares in London during the autumn of 1975 and on a couple of occasions it had affected our theatre. The audience was asked to leave half-way through a performance and we also had to go. It was amusing to see Arthur Lowe in Mainwaring style saying 'Right, follow me men', and off we would march up the road to the pub where we would have a drink before we were told that it was a false alarm, and then we would return to the theatre to continue the show. As a result of

An early Royal Performance for our 'lads' was at the BBC Television Centre in 1971. Right to Left: Vera Lynn, Eric Morecombe, Ernie Wise, Eddie Braben, Dave Allen, Huw Weldon (back to the camera), Dudley Moore, H.M. The Queen and the cast of *Dad's Army* – Ian Lavender is just out of shot.

Some of the cast being presented to H.M. The Queen and the Duke of Edinburgh after the Royal Variety Performance 1975. (*Doug McKenzie*)

these bomb scares there was a tremendous amount of security round the Palladium for the royal show.

When the weekend arrived for the royal performance we used the Shaftesbury Theatre as our base and were shuttled backwards and forwards to the Palladium by coach for rehearsal. On Sunday and Monday (the day of the show)

housed with the Rhos Male Voice Choir in a pub somewhere near – I wonder what they made of one another.

The finale of the Royal Variety performance must be as well rehearsed as any other item to ensure that the entire cast can fit on to the stage. There was Count Basie and his Band, the Rhos Male Voice Choir, Kwa Zulu dancers, the

The line-up for the final curtain rehearsal of the 1975 Royal Variety Performance: Left to Right: Harry Secombe, Vera Lynn, Michael Crawford, Telly Savalas, Count Basie, Charles Aznavour, Bruce Forsyth, and *Dad's Army*, Dukes and Lee, Kris Kremo and (behind) all other artistes taking part.
(Doug McKenzie)

we were driven back and forth along Oxford Street with packs of sandwiches and flasks of coffee. We were continually being searched and given identity papers. After we had finished the final rehearsals on Monday we were all dispersed to different buildings around the Palladium because there is only limited dressing-room accommodation there and with over three hundred and fifty people taking part in the show we could not all be accommodated. The Kwa Zulu dancers were

Billy Liar company from Drury Lane Theatre, Telly Savalas (Kojak) and his cabaret company, the cast of *Dad's Army*, plus all the other principals, Bruce Forsyth, Vera Lynn, Charles Aznavour, Dukes and Lee, Harry Secombe and the huge orchestra.

We were called over to the Palladium from our hiding place nearby just before the Royal Family arrived. We were on stage early, so had a long wait until the final curtain. We certainly saw the Duke of Edinburgh laughing at our

performance and its was an exciting moment to stand on the stage of the great theatre in front of a huge audience and in the presence of the royal couple. The entire cast were lined up after the show and introduced to her Majesty and His Royal Highness, and although it is a long evening for the performers it is equally long for them.

A moment in the evening that made me laugh was when we were waiting in the wings for the finale line-up. I was standing next to Arthur Lowe and next to him were members of the Kwa Zulu African dancers. With so many people involved, each performer is only concerned with taking his right position on the stage. On this particular occasion, Arthur and I were suddenly conscious that something was happening next to him. We looked around and saw one of the dancers next to Arthur

breast-feeding her baby. The baby and his mother's breast were level with Arthur's eye-line. Arthur did one of his double takes and then said to the lady, 'He enjoys a drink does he? I could do with one right now!'.

Other happy occasions when we were at the Shaftes-bury included celebrating Arnold Ridley's eightieth birthday. This was performed on stage with a huge cake and the national press in attend-ance. It was remarkable to think that this dear man of eighty was still playing nightly plus two matinees a week, in the theatre.

Several of the cast were invited to a tea-party at No 10 Downing Street where Prime Minister Harold Wilson was hosting a party for under-privileged children. We were greeted by Harold, his wife Mary and Marcia Williams. Several of our friends were

Arnold Ridley's 80th birthday celebration.
(PLC, London)

there, including Eric Morecombe and Ernie Wise. It was a marvellous experience to be in that historic residence and to be in the same rooms where so many great statesmen and women had been in the past. Harold Wilson made everybody feel welcome. He said to me at one stage, 'Come and sit here, this is Henry Kissinger's favourite chair.' It was wonderful to see how the prime minister together with Morecombe and Wise gave all the children their presents. Although Eric cracked plenty of jokes, Harold Wilson kept up with him and sometimes even outwitted him. Before we left Mary Wilson asked us to come and see the kitchen. It was huge, with large scrubbed tables. Mary had just made a Christmas cake and she asked us if we had children and would we like to take a slice of cake home for them. As we left No 10 I took note of all the wonderful pictures that were hanging on the staircase.

By February 1976 we were told that we would be finishing at the Shaftesbury and would be making a long tour around the country. A few items would have to be changed and the scenery altered because at times we would be playing some much smaller theatres. The orchestra was also to be reduced, but we were still going to have our wonderful musical director, Ed Coleman, with us. Clive Dunn was only doing half the tour as he had prior commitments, so Jack Haig was to play Corporal Jones when Clive left. We opened the tour at the Opera House, Manchester. The pre-publicity at the theatre left something to be desired, and for the first few days we were dashing about doing radio, newspaper and television interviews, and even dropping hand-bills into shops, which should have been handed out well before we arrived in the

city. Audiences increased after the first week and by the end of the third they were quite large. After Manchester we moved on to Blackpool which, out of season, had only a few senior citizens on holiday. We had some good social evenings in Blackpool after the performances, but that resort out of season is not exactly Las Vegas!

After Blackpool we moved to Newcastle and not only did we enjoy full houses at nearly every performance but the weather improved and it became one of the hottest summers for years. The Geordies are great people, very friendly and they like their theatre.

We played Bournemouth and some of the cast's famlies joined us there. We then moved to Birmingham and on to Nottingham, where we were able to get in some cricket practice. A match had been arranged for us to play when we arrived in Bradford so we thought we should loosen up a bit. At Nottingham we practised at the famous Trent Bridge ground, the headquarters of Nottinghamshire CC. A few of us, including eighty-year-old Arnold Ridley, had a gentle practice in the outdoor nets and then went in to the indoor cricket school. At one point Ian Lavender was bowling to me and hit me fair and square on my big toe. Brian Clough, the Nottingham Forest football manager, was also having some net practice and he drove me straight over to the football ground across the road and called the doctor to drill my toe which had already turned black. The drill did the trick and I had no after-effects.

While we were in Nottingham we were invited to a very peculiar film party after the show one night. All those invited went, with the exception of Arthur Lowe, and I reckon he must have known something. The party was in a fairly small semi-detached house and a couple of cars had been laid on to take us there. We were shown into a lounge which had a bar and a huge Hammond organ which went right up into the ceiling above. Cheese and ham rolls were handed around by the host and his wife and then their two small daughters came in and proceeded to play the enormous Hammond organ. The whole house, and probably the adjoining house next door too, shook like crazy

beat a hasty retreat out of the house and back to our hotels.

During our stay at Brighton on the Sussex coast, the theatre was completely sold out. We also had the chance to see relations and renew old acquaintances; it was pleasant for me as my wife and I with our baby son had lived in that busy resort some years earlier.

It is always enjoyable to spend a week or two in Yorkshire and this we did when we played the Bradford Alhambra. Within fifteen minutes' drive

with the vibrations, and when it finished the little girls took a bow and went to bed. The host then asked us if we would like to see some funny films. Arnold Ridley, who had been having a doze in spite of the noise of the organ, said, 'How nice, we like comedy films,' thinking of a vintage Harold Lloyd or Laurel and Hardy. It took us a few seconds to understand that the films were not to be 'funny ha! ha!', but 'funny very peculiar', so we

outside any big town in that part of the country you will find yourself in the most beautiful countryside. It was from Bradford that we travelled to play our cricket match for which we had practised in Nottingham. Arthur Lowe was President of the Hayfield Cricket Club in Derbyshire, as his father had been before him. The club wanted to build a new pavilion and the cast of *Dad's Army* were going to play Hayfield to raise the money to

Arthur Lowe inspecting his 'troops' before the cricket match at Hayfield. *(By kind permission of the Daily Mirror)*

Jeffrey Holland and family — son Sam was the reason for Jeffrey's dash to Coventry. *(Jeffrey Holland)*

make this possible. Luckily, it was a lovely sunny Sunday when we set off by coach from Bradford. The idea was to make a weekend of it, staying in various pubs in Hayfield overnight. When we arrived, the little village was seething with people who had literally turned out in their thousands 'to see their television idols', as one gentleman put it.

We all had a good lunch accompanied by plenty of the local brew. As Arthur said, 'By goom, we've stopped a few barrels going sour today.' He inspected his side before the match in military fashion and the game got under way. Every stroke played by the *Dad's Army* team drew applause from the huge crowd and a catch made by them was more than the onlookers could bear. Small boys jumped for joy and the beer tent was near to collapse as yet more beers were consumed. I was batting and had made two or three when Arnold Ridley came in and it was decided that he should have a runner. Arnold played one or two fine strokes and then became rather excited. He hit a full toss into the outfield and started to run, together with his runner and myself. We all finished up in a heap at one end and it was deemed that I was out.

At the end of the match enough money had been collected from the sale of programmes and raffles to make it possible for work to be started immediately on the new pavilion and Arthur officially opened it a year or two later. We stopped a few more barrels going sour in the evening and started off next morning for the return journey back to Bradford. Arthur was in one of his skittish moods and when the coach stopped to allow the gentlemen in the party to relieve themselves on the side of the road, hidden by the coach, Arthur quietly told the coach driver to move on. The sight of a dozen males standing in a straight line hastily adjusting their dress was like something out of a French farce.

We played the Richmond Theatre, where it had all started with those early rehearsals, and this allowed most of us to live at home that week. It also coincided with my fiftieth birthday, and as a special surprise the company had a huge cake made in the shape of my white warden's helmet. It was here at Richmond that just before the finale of the mid-week matinee that Jeffrey Holland received news that his wife had gone into labour in hospital in

Coventry. Jeffrey asked his understudy to take over for the evening show and by a miracle of good rail connections was in Coventry in two hours. As was expected it was a difficult birth, but the result was a lovely baby boy. Although Arthur Lowe quite naturally and with reason scolded Jeff on his return to the show next day for unprofessional conduct in the theatre, the first bouquet of flowers to arrive at the hospital for Jeff's wife Ellie was 'From Arthur and Joan Lowe, with love'.

The last date of the tour was at Bath and it was a most memorable finale to the six months we had been on the road after leaving the Shaftesbury Theatre in London. During the first week in Bath the Duke of Beaufort, whose famous home Badminton is not far away, brought in a party to see the show one night and asked us to have drinks with him afterwards. Among his party was Neville Chamberlain's daughter-in-law who invited us to have lunch with her and her two teenage children while we were in the city. This we did and it turned out to be a fascinating day.

Arthur Lowe and General Roosevelt admiring Neville Chamberlain's famous umbrella. *(Bath and West Evening Chronicle)*

Lunch party with Mrs Chamberlain; Left to Right: Ed Coleman, Miss Chamberlain, John Le Mesurier, Frank Williams, Arthur Lowe, General Roosevelt, Edward Sinclair, Mrs Chamberlain's mother, Master Chamberlain, Joan Lowe, the author, Marion Pertwee, Mrs Chamberlain, Tony Cundell, the author's son James (in front).
(Bath and West Evening Chronicle)

Among her guests was General Roosevelt, the late American president's son. Mrs Chamberlain's husband (Neville Chamberlain's son) had been an MP himself, but had died fairly young. Mrs Chamberlain and her children were the complete hosts that day in Bath. We were shown all the mementos concerning her father-in-law, his gifts from King George VI who was a close friend, and the letters he sent to his son during the Munich crisis in 1938. These letters were smuggled out of Germany by various means at the time and were not even trusted to the diplomatic bag. They state quite clearly that Chamberlain was buying as much time as possible because he knew that Hitler was not to be trusted. To see those actual handwritten letters concerning a period I remember so vividly as a youngster was a very extraordinary experience. Suddenly it felt as if one was back in 1938 reliving the experience of those nerve-racking days, and it made us all realise what agonising moments our parents had gone through just waiting to see what Chamberlain could do to save the country from going to war. When he arrived back in England with that piece of paper, and on the steps of the aeroplane announced that it was 'peace in our time', a huge sigh of relief went through the entire country.

We also saw and handled Chamberlain's famous brown umbrella that was his trade-mark on all those missions to Bechtesgarten. Then we had a wonderful lunch which was served on the table that was originally in the Cabinet Room at No 10 Downing Street. Before we left on that magic day we were each given a little Chamberlain souvenir.

So a year with the stage show came to an end. We however still had another television series to make before we finally said farewell to *Dad's Army*.

The Talking Wireless

Recording the radio version of *Dad's Army* was never going to be easy, but it was a very enjoyable experience and the end result was received with a great deal of pleasure by the listening public. On several occasions the recordings were done on our day off from the television studios, and there was one spell of about a fortnight when we did two recordings a day.

Writing for radio is just as difficult as writing for television. You have fifty or sixty blank pages to fill up for a half-hour programme, and in the case of *Dad's Army* it was no easier to write for radio than it was for television. Naturally the characters had been established in the public's mind for some time, but a great deal of thought had to be put into replacing the visual situations with the spoken word and to making sure that they would still be funny. One or two episodes were completely rewritten because adaptation just was not possible. Not every member of the cast was used in each programme simply because there would not have been enough for everyone to do in a particular episode.

Harold Snoad and Michael Knowles did the excellent adaptation for this very long radio series. Michael Knowles takes up the story:

❛The BBC commissioned Harold Snoad and myself to adapt *Dad's Army* for radio. They liked the pilot programme and we went on to adapt some seventy episodes.

They were recorded first at the old Playhouse Theatre in Northumberland Avenue and later at the BBC Paris Studios in Lower Regent Street. By its very nature *Dad's Army* is very visual and it required a lot of work to translate this visual element into purely sound terms. Characters were required to ascend in barrage balloons, risk death from unexploded bombs and runaway giant wheels spitting fire, commandeer trains and negotiate raging rivers while defending their country against the ever-present threat of Nazi invasion!

The producer, John Dyas, was terribly enthusiastic about the project and sometimes got a little carried away by his enthusiasm. For example, one episode had the platoon adrift in an open boat. In an attempt to simulate sitting in a rowing boat on radio John had arranged all the actors' chairs in the rough shape of a boat on the stage of the Paris Studio. This was fine in theory but it had one drawback – the microphones, which were fixed, were all on the port side of the 'boat' as it were. This meant the actors sitting on the starboard side couldn't be heard, or had to scramble over the person next to them in order to reach the microphones! This resulted in some chaos as the actors got tangled up with one another, and even in one or two cases finished up on the floor muttering mild oaths. It was then decided to go back to the more conventional broadcasting methods.

Another episode called for Clive Dunn (Corporal Jones) to cycle through the streets of Walmington-on-Sea. John Dyas decided it would be a good idea if Clive actually rode a bicycle

Song parodies were rife during the war. One of Arthur Askey's songs 'Big Hearted Arthur' was parodied in this song about air raid wardens.
'Big-Helmet Wilkie they call me,
Big-Helmet Wilkie, that's me.
Now that they've made me a warden,
I get my torch batt'ries free!
Big-Helmet Wilkie they call me,
Wilkie the Warden, that's me!
(The ARP and AFS Magazine, 1940)

on stage. Clive's enthusiastic response to this was immediate. 'I should like to volunteer to ride a bicycle round the stage, sir!' With that he leapt astride the bike and attempted several circuits of the stage before the idea was abandoned as being not only too dangerous for the cast but also for the audience! As it turned out, it worked better when Clive just walked swiftly between two microphones. Such is the magic of radio!**'**

The late John Dyas, the producer of the radio series, said at the time:

'Radio cannot hope to reproduce the visual gag, nor should it try, but when this element has been removed from any original *Dad's Army* script there remains enough dialogue for the actors to create good radio comedy. Of course the scripts cannot be performed just as they are. The visual gags have to be replaced by written lines. This was the job of the two writers. Incidentally, the two involved in this production were well known to *Dad's Army*, Harold Snoad who began as a production assistant with the television series, and Michael Knowles who took part in several episodes of the programme. They both understood the characters (and the actors playing them), created by David Croft and Jimmy Perry, well enough to make their job a little easier than it would normally have been. Re-creating their television roles for radio was no worry to the cast, but the different techniques of having to use the static microphone in a certain way to create distance and atmosphere, interspersed with all the various sound effects which have to be allowed for, took a little time but once these had been mastered our merry band of Home Guards got down to the business of entertaining, which they did terribly well.**'**

'In 1940, I was staying with my uncle and aunt at Erith in Kent. As a very young boy my uncle had been in the Boer war and had also gone through the First World War, finishing as a captain. When Anthony Eden made his radio appeal asking for Local Defence Volunteers (LDV, later the Home Guard) my uncle was the first to report to the police station offering his services. He suggested to the police sergeant that he would be most suitable to command the local platoon (shades of Mainwaring). The policeman was quick to agree. My uncle then came home and immediately decided to take all the heavy furniture out of the house, single-handed (my uncle was a big man, about six foot four inches in height). He said 'That will stop the Germans coming up the road tonight!' I had to smile when Captain Mainwaring ordered similar action during the early scenes of the feature film of Dad's Army'. Many people might have thought that this scenario was a bit too far fetched!' – Bill Pertwee.

Demob

Although rumours were flying around in the summer of 1977 that we might be recording the last series of *Dad's Army*, I don't think it made any great impression on the actors as we had heard the possibility before. However when we had the final scripts in our possession, which were all very funny with some intriguing situations, the last episode did have a certain suggestion about it that the end might be in sight. We thought that if it was the end of the series, at least we would go out on a high note and not outstay our welcome with the public who had shown so much affection for us, even including the 'baddie', Air Raid Warden Hodges.

In the entertainment business actors are always moving to pastures new and are used to change, and it has to be remembered that *Dad's Army* had lasted for nine years. The writers, Jimmy and David, had done a marathon job in creating eighty episodes altogether, as well as the feature film and stage show.

We had enjoyed the pre-filming of the last series at Thetford, the last episode of which 'Never Too Old', showed our gallant lads drinking a toast to the Home Guard and Mainwaring declaring that 'Men will always stand together whenever Britain needs them.' The episode also included the marriage of Cor-

Hodges: '**Well it's all over Mainwaring**'.
Mainwaring: '**Yes, indeed**'.
Hodges: '**I know what you're thinking**'.
Mainwaring: '**Yes, you'll have to go back to being just an ordinary greengrocer now**'.
Hodges: '**And you'll have to go back to being just an ordinary bank manager**'.
– Dialogue by Jimmy Perry and David Croft.
(Stuart Robinson)

'DAD'S ARMY'
'NEVER TOO OLD'
by
Jimmy Perry and David Croft

PRODUCER	DAVID CROFT
P.A.	GORDON ELSBURY
A.F.M.	SUSIE BELBIN
ASSISTANT	HILARY WEST
F.A.	JUDY LITTLER
	HOWARD KING
T.M.1*	BRENDAN CARR
T.M.2.	LAURIE TAYLOR
SOUND SUPERVISOR	MIKE ROBERTS
GRAMS OPERATOR	ANGELA BEVERIDGE
VISION MIXER	GEOFF POWELL
DESIGNER	MARY HUSBAND
COSTUME DESIGNER	SYLVIA THORNTON
MAKE-UP ARTIST	
CREW	16 (KEN MAJOR)

SCHEDULE

0930 - 1030		Set and Light
1030 - 1230		Camera Rehearsal
1230 - 1330		LUNCH
1330 - 1830		Camera Rehearsal with TK
1830 - 1930		DINNER
1830 - 2000		Sound and vision line-up
2000 - 2130		RECORD VTC/6HT/B1887
		on VT-23 & VT-24 & Sb2b

35mm.TK (Titles)   1500

The last script.
(BBC)

Mrs Fox with her intended, Corporal Jones. *(BBC)*

poral Jones to Mrs Fox, who, incidentally, was given away by Captain Mainwaring. So Jones had finally beaten his rivals for his sweetheart's hand.

A nice touch by David and Jimmy was to include the wives and girl-friends (those with Equity membership) of the cast to play the wedding guests. It was, in fact, the last ever episode of *Dad's Army*, and it had finished without fuss and with no dramatic ending as generally happens in television series and soap operas nowadays. The series ended quietly, just as it had started in 1968.

We had become a working family and as all families we enjoyed the social life connected with the series. Apart

'Cheers'. *(Radio Times)*

The canal trip.
(Derek Pratt)

from the social occasions already mentioned, we had several parties in our various homes and on Arthur Lowe's boat during the rehearsal and recording weeks in London. Arthur also arranged a marvellous day for us on the Regent's Canal by way of a promotion, which started off with drinks at his nearby flat. The craft we were using was quite new and a regular floating restaurant on the canal. It was a gloriously sunny day with plenty of good food and wine, and our wives were included too, which was not always possible on other occasions.

Another unusual trip was when we went to Blackpool to switch on the illuminations.

We assembled with our wives at Euston Station, and we were greeted by a gold-braided station master who showed us to our own dining car. An agreeable lunch on the train, accompanied by much conversation, eventually brought us to Blackpool in what seemed no time at all. We were given a civic welcome by the mayor, and after various media interviews we changed into our uniforms ready to throw the switch that would illumiante the famous Golden Mile. It was now pouring with rain, but the job was done very cheerily with a little assistance from a wee dram or two. We then boarded an open-top tram to make our journey, as is customary on these occasions along the 'mile'. In spite of the rain the public turned out in great numbers to cheer us on our way. The evening finished with a dinner in the company of the civic dignitaries. It had all been quite an experience.

We were asked to open a charity fête on the Isle of Wight on one occasion and some dear friends of ours, Tony and Sybil Snelling, were part of the organising committee. We had a rehearsal in London on the day in question, but David Croft allowed us to finish at mid-day. We were picked up at the BBC by a mini-bus and driven to Fairoaks Aerodrome, near Woking, where a Norman Brittain Islander aircraft was waiting to fly us to the island. The Brittain Islander was an aircraft that had been developed at Bembridge Airport for sale

around the world as an executive jet. We crowded into the aircraft on yet another wonderfully sunny day and made our way over the Surrey hills and the Hampshire coastline with glorious views of the Solent below and on to Bembridge Airport. Before landing, the pilot circled round over the area of the fête a few times, dipping his wings, and the huge crowd beneath responded by waving anything they could lay their hands on. Some of our families had gone on earlier by ferry from Portsmouth. We were met at Bembridge Airport by cars waiting to whisk us off to the venue. The crowds seemed even bigger when we got there and as well as walking round the stalls and joining in the general fun we went into a tent in shifts to sign auto-

Switching on the Blackpool illuminations.
(Blackpool Gazette)

graphs. Again with a little assistance from a tot or two accompanied by a lot of ice, because it was extremely hot. We finished the day at the Snelling residence with all sorts of edible goodies (and another tot or two!) before we were driven back to Bembridge Airport for the return flight to Fairoaks after a wonderful day.

Receiving the BAFTA award for the best situation comedy programme was a night to remember. Not only did we receive the prize from Princess Anne, but we wined and dined at London's Albert Hall in the company of some of the great entertainers of our business. Sitting on the next table to us, and there to present one of the awards, was the American film star Ray Milland, someone we had all admired and seen many times on our cinema screens. We had to wait in a tunnel, one of the many that lead up on to the

stage, and when we were called it was a memorable experience to walk on stage to the programme's signature tune 'Who do you think you are kidding Mr Hitler?' and to face the hundreds of people from our profession, and then to be introduced by Richard Attenborough to the princess. The thunderous applause which greeted our presentation was still ringing in our ears as we walked off. It was raining when we finally left

the Albert Hall at the end of the evening, but even having to wait for a taxi outside did not dampen our spirits. I was just about to step in to one with my wife when I noticed astronomer Patrick Moore also waiting with his mother. We ushered them in to our cab, and years later Patrick reminded me of this when we were playing cricket together for the Lord Taveners.

When the series did finally finish I think it slipped the

When it was suggested that we might be going to do a final series of *Dad's Army* John Laurie, who was then eighty, said, 'I'm happy to go on doing it as long as they can hold me up. If it really ends, I'll just go and be objectionable somewhere else'.

The last recording day of *Dad's Army*.

Demob party with the *Daily Mirror. (by kind permission of the Daily Mirror/Charles Ley)*

us and our wives, plus a few friends, to a sumptuous dinner at London's Café Royal, and they presented us with medals which were inscribed 'for services to television entertainment'. Speeches were made, some slightly ribald in content, and a good time was had by all. There was however more to come. We did get an invitation from the Board of Governers, no less, of the BBC at a later date to have lunch with them and compliments about the series were sincerely given and gratefully received. At the end of nine years, we had been blessed with two writers and a host of backroom boys and girls who we will always remember with great affection.

minds of the BBC hierarchy to give us the sort of send off that would have been appreciated at the time, but the *Daily Mirror* stepped in after their television critic announced the news in their columns. The *Mirror* invited

Receiving the BAFTA award (or as it was then known, SFTA) from Princess Anne. *(PLL Photos)*

Wartime Recipes

Fish in Savoury Custard

Cooking time: 45 minutes   **Quantity:** 4 helpings

4 small fillets of fish or 2 fish
  cutlets
1 egg or 1 reconstituted egg
½ pint milk

Salt and pepper
1 teaspoon chopped parsley
Small pinch mixed herbs

Method: Arrange the fillets or cutlets in a greased dish. If possible, roll the fillets. Beat the egg, pour on the milk. If using dried egg, the milk should be poured on boiling. Add seasoning, parsley and herbs. Pour over the fish and bake in a very moderate oven for approximately 45 minutes. It is advisable, as with all baked custards, to stand the dish in another containing cold water.

Pilchard Layer Loaf

Cooking time: 30 minutes,
  plus time to make sauce

Quantity: 4 helpings

1 small national wheatmeal
  loaf
1 5oz tin pilchards (4 points)
¾ pint thick white sauce
2 tablespoons vinegar

1 teaspoon mustard
salt and pepper

Method: Cut off the crusts (using them later for toast or rusks) and slice the loaf lengthwise into four. Spread each slice with pilchards mashed with a little sauce and seasoning. If the pilchards are not packed in tomato sauce you may care to add a little piquant sauce to this mixture. Dip the layers in water to moisten, then place one on top of the other to re-form a loaf. All this can be done in advance. When required, place the pilchard loaf in a fireproof dish and pour over the sauce, mixed with the mustard, vinegar and seasoning. Bake in a moderate oven for about 30 minutes. Serve with a green vegetable.

Woolton Pie

Cooking time: About 1 hour   **Quantity:** 1 helpings

This pie is named after the Minister of Food – Lord Woolton. It is an adaptable recipe that you can change according to the ingredients you have available.

Dice and cook about 1lb of each of the following in salted water: potatoes (you could use parsnips if topping the pie with mashed potatoes), cauliflower, swedes, carrots – you could add turnips too. Strain but keep ¾ pint of the vegetable water.

Arrange the vegetables in a large pie-dish or casserole. Add a little vegetable extract and about 1oz rolled oats or oatmeal to the vegetable liquid. Cook until thickened and pour over the vegetables: add 3-4 chopped spring onions.

Top with potato pastry or with mashed potatoes and a very little grated cheese and heat in the centre of a moderately hot oven until golden brown. Serve with brown gravy.

This is at its best with tender young vegetables.

Humour was always to the fore during the war years, despite the privations and hardships suffered by the armed forces and civilians alike. In Britain, food was short and you queued for everything. If you saw a line of people you joined it. One woman got in a queue and asked the lady in front of her 'What are we queuing for, ducks?'. 'The Tales of Hoffman', replied the lady. 'Blimey', said the woman, 'how do you cook them?'

Programme Titles

Title	Recording Date

1ST SERIES
Man of the Hour	15.4.68
Museum Piece	22.4.68
Command Decision	29.4.68
Enemy Within the Gates	6.5.68
The Showing Up of Corporal Jones	13.5.68
Shooting Pains	20.5.68

2ND SERIES
Operation Kilt	13.10.68
The Battle of Godfrey's Cottage	20.10.68
The Loneliness of the Long-Distance Walker	27.10.68
Sergeant Wilson's Little Secret	15.11.68
A Stripe for Frazer	15.11.68
Under Fire	27.11.68

3RD SERIES
The Armoured Might of Lance Corporal Jones	25.5.69
Battle School	1.6.69
The Lion has 'Phones	8.6.69
Something Nasty in the Vault	15.6.69
The Bullet is Not For Firing	22.6.69
Room at the Bottom	29.6.69
Big Guns	6.7.69

4TH SERIES
The Day The Balloon Went Up	23.10.69
War Dance	30.10.69
Menace From The Deep	7.11.69
Branded	14.11.69
Man Hunt	21.11.69
No Spring for Frazer	28.11.69
Sons of the Sea	5.12.69

5TH SERIES
Sergeant – Save My Boy	27.6.70
Don't Fence Me In	10.7.70
The Big Parade	17.7.70
Don't Forget the Diver	24.7.70
Boots Boots Boots	31.7.70
Absent Friends	7.8.70

6TH SERIES
Put That Light Out	30.10.70
The Two and a Half Feathers	6.11.70
Mum's Army	13.11.70
The Test	20.11.70
A. Wilson (Manager)	27.11.70
Unwanted Guests	4.12.70
Fallen Idol	11.12.70

SPECIAL
Battle of the Giants   19.9.71

7TH SERIES
Getting the Bird   19.5.72
Asleep in the Deep   26.5.72
Soldier's Farewell   2.6.72
Keep Young and Beautiful   9.6.72
The Desperate Drive of Lance Corporal Jones   16.6.72
The King Was In His Counting House   23.6.72
If the Cap Fits . . .   30.6.72

8TH SERIES
All Is Safely Gathered In   3.11.72
When Did You Last See Your Money?   10.11.72
Brain Versus Brawn   17.11.72
Brush With The Law   26.11.72
Round and Round Went the Great Big Wheel   1.12.72
Time On My Hands   8.12.72

9TH SERIES
My British Buddy   8.6.73
We Know Our Onions   15.6.73
The Deadly Attachment   22.6.73
The Royal Train   29.6.73
The Honourable Man   8.7.73
Things That Go Bump in the Night   15.7.73
The Recruit   22.7.73

10TH SERIES
Man of Action   7.5.74
Godiva Affair   3.11.74
Turkey Dinner   10.11.74
The Captain's Car   17.11.74
Everybody's Trucking   27.10.74
Gorilla Warfare   27.10.74

11TH SERIES
My Brother and I   23.5.75
High Finance   30.5.75
When You've Got To Go   6.6.75
Is There Honey Still For Tea?   26.6.75
Ring Dem Bells   3.7.75
Come In, Your Time Is Up   10.7.75
The Face On The Poster   17.7.75

SPECIAL
The Love of Three Oranges   10.12.76

12TH SERIES
The Miser's Hoard   24.6.77
The Making of Private Pike   1.7.77
Make-Up Walmington   8.7.77
Number Engaged   15.7.77
Knights of Madness   22.7.77
Never Too Old   29.7.77

Acknowledgements:

This work could obviously not have been compiled without Jimmy Perry and David Croft. After all DAD'S ARMY was their original baby, and I do appreciate their help with this publication.

Joan Lowe had the foresight, thank goodness, to put diary type notes into print, which gave me a great insight into Arthur's career.

Joan Le Mesurier, Althea Ridley, Kay Back and Gladys Sinclair very kindly gave me their unstinted help.

Ian Lavender reminded me of amusing moments which I had forgotten, and Clive Dunn, during various phone calls from his home in Portugal, was able to put me right on certain facts.

Frank Williams laughed a lot when we met to talk about the show, but then Frank always did laugh a lot!

To everyone I bothered with phone calls and/or letters, my sincere apologies, and grateful thanks for their response with information and pictures.

I would like to thank the Bell and Anchor Hotels at Thetford. Harold Snoad has a phenomenal memory and was able to recall many anecdotes, particularly in the earlier years of the television production.

For permission to use their pictures, thank you Brian Fisher, Woman Magazine, my good friend Doug McKenzie, Lynn News, Jon Kimble and the Daily Mirror, Michael Fresco, Columbia Tristar Pictures and National Screen Services, and The Blackpool Gazette. Thanks also to Punch for permission to reproduce three of their cartoons.

I am indebted to Norman Longmate's fascinating book *The Real Home Guard* (Hutchinson Library Services).

Thanks to photographers Dawson Strange, Cobham, Surrey, for their very prompt and efficient service rendered at short notice.

My thanks to John Bridger at BBC Enterprises for his help. Some spot editing had to be carried out when I was writing, and as time was precious I'm grateful to my wife Marion for her help in this.

I must give a very special thank you to Geraldine Guthrie who deciphered my dreadful handwriting and produced a fine finished presentation for the publishers. Robert Wiltshire did a great job producing the colour slides from, in some cases, rather old and faded photos. Christopher Dowling and his staff at the Imperial War Museum conveyed their enthusiasm and help at an early stage in the project, for which I am most grateful. The recipes on p.141 come from a collection of wartime recipes at the Imperial War Museum.

To my business manager and publicist Tony Mulliken at PMP Management, thanks mate!

I have tried very hard to contact all the various sources of photographs. Several of these carried no identification and therefore I have not been able to credit the photographs, for this I apologise.

My special thanks to Beverly Smith for her hard work and helpful suggestions in putting the finishing touches to the book and to Gillian Matthews at Parke Sutton for visual layouts.

This is my third publication with David and Charles, and it's always a pleasure to visit them in Newton Abbot.

'Over four years ago, in May 1940, our country was in mortal danger. The most powerful army the world had ever seen had forced its way to within a few miles of our coast. From day to day we were threatened with invasion.

For most of you — and, I must add, for your wives too — your service in the Home Guard has not been easy. Some of you have stood for many hours on the gun sites, in desolate fields, or wind-swept beaches. Many of you, after a long and hard day's work, scarcely had time for food before you changed into uniform for the evening parade. Some of you had to bicycle for long distances to the drill hall or the rifle range...

But you have gained something for yourselves. You have discovered in yourselves new capabilities. You have found how men from all kinds of homes and many different occupations can work together in a great cause, and how happy they can be with each other. I am very proud of what the Home Guard has done and I give my heartfelt thanks to you all ... I know that your country will not forget that service' — King George VI, radio broadcast, *Sunday 3 December 1944*